QUALITY AUDITS FOR IMPROVED PERFORMANCE

Also available from ASQ Quality Press

Audit Standards: A Comparative Analysis, Second Edition
Walter Willborn

*Standard Manual of Quality Auditing: A Step-by-Step Workbook
with Procedures and Checklists*
Greg Hutchins

*How to Make the Most of Every Audit: An Etiquette Handbook
for Auditing*
Charles B. Robinson

How to Plan an Audit
ASQC Quality Audit Technical Committee; Charles B. Robinson, editor

To request a complimentary catalog of publications, call 800-248-1946.

QUALITY AUDITS FOR IMPROVED PERFORMANCE

Second Edition

Dennis R. Arter

ASQ Quality Press
Milwaukee, Wisconsin

Quality Audits for Improved Performance, Second Edition
Dennis R. Arter

Library of Congress Cataloging-in-Publication Data

Arter, Dennis R.
　　Quality audits for improved performance / Dennis R. Arter.—2nd
　ed.
　　　p.　cm.
　　Includes index.
　　ISBN 0-87389-263-1
　　1. Quality control—Auditing.　I. Title.
　TS156.A76　1994
　658.5'62—dc20　　　　　　　　　　　　　　　　　　　93-46980
　　　　　　　　　　　　　　　　　　　　　　　　　　　CIP

© 1994 by ASQ

10 9 8 7

ISBN 0-87389-263-1

Acquisitions Editor: Susan Westergard
Project Editor: Jeanne Bohn
Production Editor: Annette Wall
Marketing Administrator: Mark Olson
Set in Janson Text by Linda J. Shepherd.
Cover design by Montgomery Media, Inc.
Printed and bound by BookCrafters, Inc.

ASQ Mission:　To facilitate continuous improvement and increase customer satisfaction by identifying, communicating, and promoting the use of quality principles, concepts, and technologies; and thereby be recognized throughout the world as the leading authority on, and champion for, quality.

For a free copy of the ASQ Quality Press Publications Catalog, including ASQ membership information, call 800-248-1946.

Printed in the United States of America

 Printed on acid-free recycled paper

American Society for Quality

Quality Press
611 East Wisconsin Avenue
Milwaukee, Wisconsin 53202
Call toll free 800-248-1946
www.asq.org
http://qualitypress.asq.org
http://standardsgroup.asq.org
http://e-standards.asq.org
E-mail: authors@asq.org

Contents

Preface

You are about to be introduced to some old and some new approaches to the application of management audits. In today's environment of intense global competition, the old adversarial methods of seek, point, and blame will no longer work. Using some of the basic financial audit principles (thus the term *audit*), we can examine the usefulness and implementation of management controls as they apply to internal and external operations. Management audits, along with other forms of evaluation, are now being used successfully by organizations as a means of determining whether their own controls and their supplier controls work effectively.

Since this text was first published in 1989, some changes in auditing have taken place. Little did I realize then how much of an effect the international quality standards, ISO 9000, would have on American business and government. As a result of the general acceptance of these basic ISO 9000 quality concepts, interest in auditing has exploded. With this intense interest in auditing, new ideas and techniques are being developed. The published literature has doubled in size and tripled in content. With this new excitement, I have also discovered some underlying truths, which I hope to impart in this revision.

Two important changes have occurred in this revision.

- The concept of audit findings and observations has been modified.
- The concept of product audits has been removed.

In my travels I have discovered that many groups misuse the audit *observation*. I had originally presented an observation as a minor problem, or a precursor to a major problem. I found, instead, that people were parking miscellaneous matters in this category. If it was too hard to analyze, it was called an observation. This is, of course, wrong. As a result, I have removed *observation* from the adverse conclusion category. I now use it as it is presented in the ISO 10011 auditing standard: a fact (good or bad) gathered during an audit.

As for the so-called product audit, it has become more and more apparent that this was an inspection. One would take finished items or subassemblies and subject them to examination. Although this could theoretically evaluate the inspection process, in reality it was a fancy, and often expensive, inspection. I have dropped it from the list of management audit types.

Acknowledgments

Four major forces have influenced me during the past 20 years. Management principles were first learned in the U.S. Navy nuclear submarine force. Upon leaving the navy I developed my basic audit skills while employed by a nuclear power utility. Although I had some help from the existing consensus standards, it was mainly a trial and error process. I made several mistakes, but I learned from those mistakes. I started training others in audit methods through the use of a package course developed in 1978 by Mr. Frank X. Brown for the U.S. Department of Energy. Seeing a need for auditing in a nonregulated commercial environment, I struck out on my own as a consultant in the fall of 1984. Since then, I continue to learn from each company I visit and each class I teach.

Membership in the Quality Audit Division of the American Society for Quality Control has had a great deal of influence on my perception of many of the concepts presented in this book. Development of the fundamental principles of auditing was influenced by the Institute of Internal Auditors and, of course, by Larry Sawyer.

The area of auditing, in its many forms, is acknowledged by business and government as a cost-effective means of improving quality. The methods described in this book are both old and new. Because they challenge old paradigms, they will cause controversy. They may be difficult to accept and even more difficult to implement. They do, however, work. This book will cause you to think. Enjoy!

Chapter 1

Introduction

What Is an Audit?

Although many people use the term *audit,* it is not always applied in a consistent manner. This is because people use words based on their previous experiences or what they have read. The word *audit* originally comes from the practice of recording the cargo on a ship by aurally hearing the captain call out the items and quantities. The auditor represented the king and was there to provide assurance that all taxes on that cargo would be properly recorded.[1] So, from the very beginning, auditors were associated with controls and compliance. Gradually, others used the process of having an outsider provide assurances to the interested parties. Now, we have quality auditors, financial auditors, safety auditors, tax auditors, and many more. All of these auditing schemes can be divided into two categories: compliance and management.

A compliance audit looks for conformance to a set of rules. The rules may not be questioned; they are set. Examples of compliance audits include the following:

> • *Tax audits.* These are performed by revenue agents at the local, state, and national level. They check to see that taxes are reported and paid in accordance with the tax codes.

- *Financial audits.* These are the traditional audits of accounting controls, such as accounts payable, accounts receivable, and payroll. They are performed internally, within a company, or externally, on another company. They give assurances to management and stockholders that the balance sheets and income statements are accurate. They are also designed to prevent (or minimize) waste, fraud, and abuse.

- *Regulatory audits.* Certain activities of society are regulated by the government. Among these are the production of energy, the stewardship of the environment, the production of food, the protection of workers, and the use of medical devices. The health and safety of consumers are of prime importance in these regulated areas. Laws are passed and regulations are promulgated. Auditors verify that these laws and regulations are being implemented.

- *High-risk audits.* For some events the consequences of failure are unacceptable. These include the operation of airplanes and submarines, and the launching of rockets to the moon. A complete and thorough audit of the finished product is necessary before it is activated or placed into service. Auditors check inspection records, craft qualification records, design review records, and other forms of proof.

Compliance audits are designed to give assurance that activities have been performed properly. By their very nature, they are reactive (not proactive). One does not question the *rules*. One only looks for compliance to those rules. These audits are binary—pass or fail.

A management audit looks for both conformance with a set of rules and the effectiveness of those rules in achieving an organization's goals. Here the rules are challenged, but the basic requirements are not. Examples of management audits are as follows:

- *Quality audits.* These are performed to analyze the effectiveness and implementation of programs designed to maximize the quality of goods or services delivered to the customer.

- *Environmental, Safety, and Health (ES&H) audits.* Just as the quality of the product is important, workplace safety and environmental stewardship are also important. Auditors can provide assurances to management that their ES&H programs are working.

- *Operational audits.* These audits are performed by internal auditors, normally working in the controller or accounting department. They examine reliability and integrity of information; compliance with policies, plans, procedures, laws, and regulations; the safeguarding of assets; economical and efficient use of resources; and accomplishment of established objectives.[2]

- *Government program audits.* Government agencies have a mission to serve the citizens and the legislators. On the federal level each cabinet agency has an inspector general organization, charged with monitoring the effectiveness of that agency in the performance of its mission. The Congress also has the General Accounting Office (GAO) to examine the effectiveness of government operations.[3]

Although this text will concentrate on quality audits, the principles apply to any type of management (or analog) assessment. There is no valid reason to separate management auditing into subcomponents. Management is the control of resources. The goals of quality, safety, environmental stewardship, and efficiency are all driven by the same set of rules: define requirements, produce to those requirements, monitor achievement of those requirements, and continuously improve on the requirements.

Audit Defined

The Quality Auditing Technical Committee (now Quality Audit Division) of the American Society for Quality Control has defined an *audit* as

> A planned, independent, and documented assessment to determine whether agreed-upon requirements are being met.[4]

The international auditing standard, ISO 10011 (Guidelines for Auditing Quality Systems), defines a *quality audit* as

> A systematic and independent examination to determine whether quality activities and related results comply with planned arrangements and whether these arrangements are implemented effectively and are suitable to achieve objectives.[5]

Contained in the definition of the quality audit are two important concepts: compliance with written requirements (planned arrangements) and effectiveness of those requirements in meeting basic management controls. Auditing may be thought of as the process of comparing reality with requirements. This comparison results in an evaluation to management. Managers want to know if their requirements are achieving the necessary controls. Quality auditors provide them with that knowledge (Figure 1.1).

This comparison process can be accomplished by three different sets of auditors and auditees: first party, second party, and third party. The *first-party* audit, also known as an *internal audit*, is performed within your own company. This can be a central office group auditing one of the plants, auditing within a division, local audits within the plant, or any number of similar combinations. There are no external customer-supplier audit relationships here, just internal customers and suppliers.

The *second-party* audit is performed by a customer on a supplier. A contract is in place and goods are being, or will be, delivered. If you are in the process of approving a potential supplier through the application of these auditing techniques, you are performing a *supplier survey.* A survey is performed before the contract is signed; an audit is performed after the contract is signed. Second-party audits are also called *external audits,* if you are the one doing the auditing. If you are being audited by your customer, that operation is still a second-party audit, but, since you are now on the receiving end, it is called an *extrinsic audit.*

A *third-party* audit is performed by someone other than the customer, on a supplier or regulated entity. The party to be audited will hire someone to audit them. They may subsequently use the results of that audit as a marketing tool. (This assumes that the results of the third-party audit are favorable!) The most common type of third-party audit is an ISO 9000 registration audit. (Other countries use the term *certification* rather than

Figure 1.1. Are management controls present and working?

registration.) Regulated industries, such as nuclear power stations and medical device manufacturers, have government representatives perform audits on their operations to provide assurances of safety to the public.

Management Principles

Regardless of the goods or services produced, all management systems include four fundamental activities.

Planning

The activities to be performed should be planned before they happen. Responsibilities must be set so that accountability and ownership of resulting performance is established. The identity and needs of the customer should be defined. Requirements should be specified in written documents that are used to describe the work activity or products ordered. All the requirements and documents become the base against which quality is measured.

Performance

The action should proceed as planned. Records should be kept so that measurement can take place. Those performing the tasks should be given the proper tools and training to accomplish the job as specified.

Measurement

The success (or failure) of an activity needs to be measured against some accepted standard. Tools used include inspection, surveillance, audit, appraisal, evaluation, and review. All involved in the activity should be aware of the quality as measured. Feedback from the customer is vital to success.

Improvement

Problems must be corrected and the process improved. Managers and workers can share concepts for improvement, but the ultimate responsibility for such improvement rests with management (line officials). Changes should be communicated to the customer.

These are the fundamental building blocks for any management control system. Often referred to as the P-D-C-A cycle (Plan-Do-Check-Act), these blocks are basic to any Total Quality Management approach (Figure 1.2). Managers select people capable of creating a good product or service. They then ensure that the employees are properly trained, equipped, motivated, and supervised to achieve the desired delivered quality. Using the framework of Total Quality Management, managers can perform their traditional duties of planning, organizing, directing, and controlling.

Fundamental Rules for Auditing

It can be seen from the above discussion on management concepts that auditing deals with the last two steps in the P-D-C-A cycle: measuring and improving. There can be no audit unless requirements have been developed. Likewise, some activity must have taken place in order to measure the implementation of those requirements.

In order to provide managers with the knowledge they desire, quality audits must follow these five basic standards:

1. *Auditing is a function of management.*
2. *Auditors are qualified to perform their tasks.*
3. *Measurements are taken against defined standards.*
4. *Conclusions are based on fact.*
5. *Audit reports focus on the control system.*

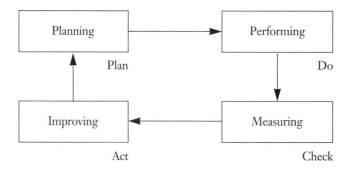

Figure 1.2. The quality cycle.

Each of these basic concepts will be discussed in greater detail in subsequent chapters.

A Different Philosophy

To be useful, audits must be performed and presented in a meaningful fashion. Peter Drucker, the well-known author of several books on management principles, has said that workers work in the system, while managers work on the system. In order for the affected managers to work on the process being audited, results must be in management's terms and appeal to their interests. Do they really care if six 5391 Forms are missing the Shift Supervisor's signature? So what? If, however, your audit is performed such that a projection of the continued practice of not recording reviews shows that the quality of the maintenance program is or could be adversely affected, then the responsible managers can take steps to correct the situation. Or perhaps this was just a bad day for an otherwise excellent employee, and represents no real threat. Management can then turn its attention to more important matters.

A different perspective for management-type audits is needed. Instead of examining past conformance to requirements and regulations in minute detail, you can use current performance to project future actions. It is better to avoid dwelling on mistakes of the past. They can never be changed. A backward looking view cannot achieve the goal of improved performance within the organization being examined. It will only lead to antagonism and back-stabbing. This is because people are powerless to change the past. They become frustrated and strike back, usually at you. Instead, use past practices to predict future performance, which can be changed.

Modern management audits should be a combination of compliance and effectiveness evaluations. Using defined and agreed-to measurement criteria, the audit report will tell managers the following:

- Whether controls exist and are adequate
- Whether controls are being implemented
- Whether controls really work

The only way to successfully meet these needs is to thoroughly prepare for the audit, conduct the evaluation with a high degree of professionalism, and present the report in terms meaningful to management. Then your customers, using the information presented by the audit report, will be able to make changes to improve future performance.

Notes

1. Sawyer, Lawrence B. *The Practice of Modern Internal Auditing*, 2nd ed. (Altamonte Springs, Fla.: Institute of Internal Auditors, 1981): 3.

2. *Standards for the Practice of Internal Auditing* (Altamonte Springs, Fla.: Institute of Internal Auditors, 1978): 6.

3. *Generally Accepted Government Auditing Standards* (Washington, D.C.: U.S. General Accounting Office, 1988).

4. *Certified Quality Auditor Brochure* (Milwaukee, Wis.: American Society for Quality Control, June 1991): 8.

5. *ISO 10011-1:1990, Guidelines for Quality Systems Audits* (Geneva: International Standards Organization, 1990): 1.

Chapter 2

Preparation

Phases of the Audit Process

Auditing may be divided into four phases, progressing sequentially through the process that was discussed in chapter 1.

1. The preparation phase starts from the decision to conduct an audit. It includes all activities from team selection up to the on-site gathering of information.

2. The performance phase begins with the on-site opening meeting and includes the gathering of information and analysis of that information. Normally, this is accomplished by conducting interviews, watching activities, and examining items and records.

3. The reporting phase covers the translation of the audit team's conclusions into a tangible product. It includes the exit meeting with managers and publication of the formal audit report.

4. The closure phase deals with the actions resulting from the report and the recording of the entire effort. For audits resulting in the identification of some weakness, the closure phase includes tracking and evaluating the follow-up action taken by others to fix the problem and keep it from repeating. Often, this part of the closure phase is referred to as corrective action.

Steps in the Preparation Phase

Between the time you receive an assignment and the time the audit starts, there are many things to be done to lay the foundation and properly organize the work. The experienced auditor probably does it routinely from habit. The novice tends to do a great deal of fumbling in an audit before getting down to the actual surveys and examinations. To minimize such fumbling, you should use the following nine steps for preparation:

1. Define the purpose of the audit.
2. Define the scope of the audit.
3. Determine the audit team resources to be used.
4. Identify the authority for the audit.
5. Identify the performance standards to be used.
6. Develop a technical understanding of the processes to be audited.
7. Contact those to be audited.
8. Perform an initial evaluation of lower-tier documents to higher-level requirements.
9. Develop written checklists of the data needs.

While each audit is likely to be different from the others, these steps are common to all, regardless of where you will be and what programs will be examined. Just as airline pilots use a preflight checklist to verify that all items have been accomplished prior to takeoff, you may need to check a list before your own takeoff. Such a reminder list is not designed to inhibit your creativity; it will merely make the planning easier. Any format will do nicely, as long as it contains the items to accomplish and some due dates. (The nine steps mentioned above would be the minimum.) Once the list is prepared, you may proceed with an assurance that important actions will not be forgotten.

Purpose

What do you and your customers want to achieve with the audit? The answer to this question is critically important to the success of an audit and, thus, improved performance. However, in order to define the needs, you must first define the customers.

When you perform audits, you have three basic customers (Figure 2.1).

- The auditee
- The client
- The organization

Each of these three customers must be defined and analyzed.

The people being audited are perhaps the most important customers. They will be working with you in the data-gathering (fieldwork) efforts and they are most directly affected by your actions and your product. In official auditing terms, these people are called *the auditee*.

You must also serve the person who just gave you this auditing assignment. This is the person in charge of the audit function—the audit boss. In official auditing terms, this person is called *the client*.

For first-party audits, the client might be the quality assurance manager or the technical services manager. For second-party audits, the client might be the purchasing manager or the procurement quality manager. For third-party audits, the client is someone in the registering company or the regulatory agency.

The client should be one person and not a committee. Someone needs to be in charge of the auditors. Someone must be responsible and accountable for the actions of the auditors. This accountability cannot be delegated or spread around a group.

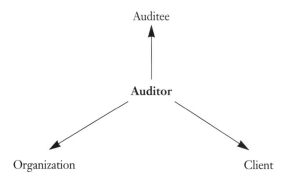

Figure 2.1. Customers of the auditor.

The final customer of the auditor is the organization as a whole. Practices, concepts, and even profits are all affected by your audit. You will have an influence on the functioning of your company or agency. For external audits of your suppliers, you represent your company to the outside world. They will see the company as you.

Of course, all three customers of the audit (auditee, client, and organization) ultimately serve the external customer. When preparing for the audit, it is useful to picture the three internal customers and the external customer. Attach some names to these pictures. Then ask yourself, "What are their needs? How can I, the auditor, meet those needs?" This is a tall order, but very important to successful auditing.

As discussed in chapter 1, embodied in the concept of management audits are two fundamental questions.

- Are the control systems any good? (Adequacy/Effectiveness)
- Are the control systems being used? (Implementation)

These two questions form the foundation of every quality audit. They must always be addressed in the purpose statement for your audit assignment. For internal (first-party) audits the purpose is normally associated with improving existing operations: reducing scrap, preventing lost time from accidents, shortening design to production cycles, and other business issues. For external (second-party) audits the primary purpose is to provide confidence in the quality of the goods and services delivered to your company, the purchaser. You must be assured that your supplier's internal control systems are working. For the third-party audit the users of the report are buying your expertise to evaluate the strength of the auditee's management. Notice that all of these thoughts ultimately return to the concept of comparing and analyzing actions to promises.

Management audits must examine both the compliance with, and the effectiveness of, existing control methods. Your customers (users of the audit report) truly wish to know whether controls are being followed and whether those controls are working as planned.

This leads us to the first of five basic *Rules* for quality audits.

1. Auditing is a function of management.

You, the auditor, act as an extension of the management function. You are the eyes, ears, and brain of management. Whether you perform audits internally or externally, you are being hired to think like a manager.

Once you have determined the purpose of the audit, write it down. Each audit should have a unique purpose; this is not something that is generated once and then recycled again and again. The generation of this unique purpose statement forces you, the auditor, to think about the task to be accomplished and the needs of your customers. Normally, the purpose statement is one or two sentences long.

> The purpose of this audit is to evaluate the adequacy and implementation of internal HACCP controls in meeting food manufacturing safety requirements.

Scope

Your next step in the preparation phase is to establish the scope of the audit. The scope establishes your boundaries and identifies the items, groups, and activities to be examined. Defining the scope also helps to make the most efficient use of limited audit resources.

When planning audits, one should also consider the time resources of the people being audited. Remember, production and staff assignments will be adversely affected as you disrupt a set routine.

Process Audits

The process audit examines an activity to verify that the inputs, actions, and outputs are in accordance with defined requirements. It covers only a portion of the total program and should take a relatively short period of time. This type of audit checks the conformance of all aspects of the process to defined requirements. It also examines the adequacy and effectiveness of the process. Many organizations refer to a process audit as a *surveillance* or a *mini-audit* to distinguish it from the much larger system audit discussed below.

The boundary of a process audit should be a single process, such as marking, stamping, cooking, coating, or installing. It is very focused and usually involves only one work crew. Process audits will have their boundaries defined by traditional process affectors: methods, material, machinery, manpower, measurement, and environment. Some of you may know these as cause and effect (or fishbone) parameters.

The process audit is normally completed in less than two hours. The results of this short process examination are reported in something less than one page. As you move away from inspection and toward Total Quality Management, the process audit (surveillance) becomes an important tool in the achievement of quality.

System Audits

A system audit is known by several other names, including management audit, management review, operational audit, supplier survey, program audit, program evaluation, business review, and various substitutions of the terms *review* and *assessment* for the word *audit*. It is characterized by its examination of the bigger picture of the organization and/or project. The application and effectiveness of system controls for effective program management are the domain of the system audit.

System audits, by their nature, will have much larger boundaries. They often cross organizational, process, and product boundaries. Examples include one or more of the following:

- Product lines
- Process areas
- Functional departments
- Quality systems
- Manufacturing locations
- Customers
- Specific projects
- Time

A system audit might examine the maintenance system, the training system, the quality circle system, the drawing control system, or the order entry system. System audits can be extremely damaging if done incorrectly, but they can be extremely beneficial when done correctly.

The scope of an audit has a significant effect on the resources and time requirements for your audit. If the scope is too large, the audit cannot possibly be completed in a reasonable time. Conversely, too narrow a scope will waste valuable resources. Economics and personnel availability must also be considered when developing the scope. System audits that are greater than one week in duration for the performance (data gathering) phase are normally excessive. On the other hand, if the performance phase is less than a day, your return on investment (planning time and energy) is small.

As you might imagine, process audits will always be internal (first-party) audits. Unless part of the bigger picture, you would not conduct a process audit on your supplier; that is their job. System audits may be first-party, second-party, or third-party audits. For best results, your internal audits should be a mix of about 75 percent process audits and 25 percent system audits.

Keeping track of the audit scope may be one of the more challenging tasks for the audit team. Often during the course of an audit, additional areas in need of examination appear that may be outside of the original scope of the audit. You must ask yourself whether the concern is important enough to pursue immediately, or whether it can wait for a separate examination at a later date. Consult with your team leader or your audit manager for suggestions. Generally, it's best to stick to the original scope, regardless of what develops. You will be perceived as more credible when you stick to the rules. Additionally, you probably lack the necessary preparation for that new area, leading to a poor job of investigation.

Does this mean that the audit team should ignore a serious deficiency, uncovered during the course of their audit, just because it lies outside of the current scope? Of course not. You should proceed as you would under a non-audit situation. Use the established methods already in place (e.g., problem report, nonconformance report, or trouble desk) to report the condition to those managers that are affected. You have done your duty and can now proceed with the audit as planned. If the deficient area warrants additional, in-depth examination, suggest that it be placed on the audit schedule as a special audit.

The Audit Team

In theory, the next step is to select the audit team, based on the purpose and scope just developed. In practice, the resources of the audit group will often determine the purpose and scope. Only so many audits can be performed by a staff of two. Only so many suppliers can be examined when travel funds are limited.

Who should I use for this audit? is an important question. The success or failure of your audit could depend on the composition of the audit team. It is reasonable to insist that audits be performed in an unbiased manner by people who have knowledge of that auditing task. The first condition requires that the auditors lack a vested interest in that which is being audited. The second condition requires the auditors to be qualified in the process of auditing.

Independence

It is often said that auditors must be independent of that which is to be audited. In fact, the definition of quality auditing found in ISO 10011-1:1990 refers to an *independent examination*. The idea is to allow the auditor to say the things that must be said, without fear of reprisal. However, total independence is rarely achievable and will often lead to ineffective audits. A totally independent person knows little about the subject being audited. First-party (internal) auditors can never be totally independent; they are paid by the company they are auditing. Second-party (external and extrinsic) auditors cannot be totally independent, as supplier quality will determine a company's quality, and thus success in the marketplace. Even third-party (registration) auditors cannot be independent, as they are under contract to the company being audited. These difficulties can be overcome by requiring the auditors to be free of a vested interest in the area to be audited. They must not own the very thing being audited. It cannot be their creation. Their performance ratings cannot depend on the success or failure of the project to be audited. They cannot be in charge of the group to be audited. Referring to the ISO 10011 auditing standard again, "Auditors should be free from bias and influences which could affect objectivity." [1]

Continuous use of one-person audits is an invitation to trouble. To prevent your audit program from becoming a narrow interpretation of existing standards or methods, you need more than one auditor. No matter how well you plan or how clear the standards appear, the job will always require some interpretation. A single auditor will eventually steer those being audited down his or her path of goodness. While you may be blessed with a good deal of talent, eventually this single perspective will cause pain.

Although audits by an individual are allowed by the auditing standards, the multiple auditor approach encourages balance and will be assumed for the duration of this text. For the larger, system audits you should have a team of at least two auditors. The person in charge of the team is called the *team leader* or *lead auditor*. Those on the team are referred to as *team members* or *auditors*. Any team with more than six members, however, becomes a mob. It cannot be controlled effectively, even by the experienced team leader.

The smaller, process audit, will normally be performed by one person. However, you should have more than one person performing a series of many process audits all around the plant. Some companies put their process audits under the direction of individual department managers. On any given day, one or two process audits will be occurring in each department around the plant.

People from outside the traditional QA/QC functions should be considered as part of the audit program resources. It may be common for the team leader of a system audit to be a quality analyst or lead lab technician. However, audit team members can, and should, be drawn from both line and staff functions within the organization. You could start by looking back at the purpose and scope. Then invite experts to join the team as part-time helpers. These other team members could include training specialists, secretaries, maintenance technicians, buyers, engineers, and even managers from another group. Other hourly employees from a related discipline may make ideal team members, as they often see the controls being examined from a different perspective and become champions for the defined controls after the audit is finished.

The makeup of auditors for the smaller, process audits is easier to determine. All of the above-mentioned people are candidates for process auditors. Salaried, as well as hourly, people should be used for process auditing. The only serious limitation is the caution against vested interest.

Qualification

Auditors must be qualified to perform their task. This is contained in the definition of auditor, found in ISO 10011-1:1990: "A person who has the qualification to perform quality audits." This qualification is composed of three elements.

1. Knowledge of the process of auditing
2. Technical knowledge of the processes to be audited
3. Ability to communicate, both orally and in writing

It is a good idea to record the qualification of each auditor on a piece of paper, often called a *certificate*. This attests to another person that the auditor possesses the necessary skills to do his or her job. Each time you audit, expect others to ask you for your auditor certification papers; they have the right to expect decent auditors. Whenever you get audited, ask the auditors for their papers.

All of this discussion on independence and qualification leads us to the second of five basic *Rules* for quality audits:

2. Auditors are qualified to perform their tasks.

Authority

The next step in the preparation phase is to verify your authority to perform the audit. One reason for identifying this authority is to defuse the natural human reaction to become defensive when informed of a forthcoming audit. Some may even develop the opinion that they are being harassed. By specifying the authority for the audit to all involved parties (including your client and other users of the audit), you confer legitimacy to the audit and remove (or minimize) those adverse feelings. Of course, another reason to verify your authority is to avoid wasting time preparing for something not authorized.

Your authority to perform internal (first-party) audits should reside in the document describing your quality assurance program. For most companies, this is something called a *Quality Assurance Manual.* This document should define the authority of certain individuals or groups to perform either process or system audits, or both. When you are reviewing the authority statements, be sure to verify that the area you wish to audit is included. Many companies will claim, "People are our most important resources." Yet, the human resources group is not on the list of those functions to be audited. Sure, production is included, but have you included marketing and sales? These are all contributors to the quality of your product (as seen by the customers) and they should be audited.

Your authority to perform external (second-party) audits should reside in the purchasing agreements between you and the supplier. This is normally a contract or purchase order. Sometimes this authority is hidden in a fine print, oftentimes under the *rights of access* heading. Federal government agencies are required by the Federal Acquisition Regulations to include this authority in most procurement documents.

What if the authority to do a supplier audit is not in the contract? (For older contracts this is probably the case.) It is generally best to continue preparation for the audit, but bring this deficiency to the attention of the responsible buyer, so it may be corrected in the next contract change.

If your authority to perform internal audits is missing, you should not be doing audits yet. One of the requirements for an audit program is to have standards against which measurements are taken. If the audit procedure is missing, then other procedures are also probably missing. Write the other procedures first.

Performance Standards

Standards are the norms or criteria against which the performance of an activity is measured. They are one of the two major inputs to the process of auditing, as discussed earlier. One cannot audit without performance standards.

Performance standards come in four levels (Figure 2.2). At the top (level 1) are those policy documents that cannot, and must not, be challenged. Examples of level 1 documents include corporate policy statements, international and national quality system standards (for example, ISO 9001 or ANSI/ASQC Q9001), regulatory standards (for example, nuclear or medical device), and business sector standards (for example, CMA's Responsible Care™). These standards give broad policy requirements, such as *implement a system of internal audits,* but do not give direction on how to accomplish these requirements.

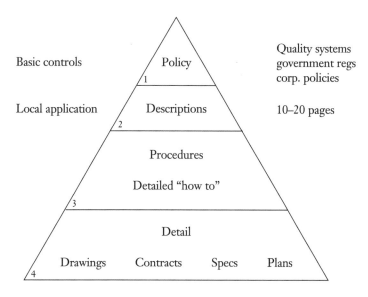

Figure 2.2. Document levels.

The next level of performance standards is the transition document between policy (level 1) and procedures (level 3). These transition documents should be relatively skinny and are often called *manuals*. There may be several of these transition documents, one for each section, department, or division. The corporate manual could be called level 2a, while the plant manual could be called level 2b. Other countries refer to these levels as tiers, but the concept is the same.

It should be noted that a binder filled with many procedures does not fall under this definition of a manual. The level 2 manual should be narrative in its writing style, as if you were talking to your neighbor. It describes how the requirements of level 1 will be implemented at a particular location. The detailed, step-by-step, process of accomplishing the task is reserved for the level 3 procedure. A good size for a level 2 manual is 20–30 pages.

The third level of performance standards is the procedure. It is in the procedure that one finds the step-by-step requirements for the job. Procedures must be clear, correct, and effective. They must provide direction to a trained individual on the performance of the job. You will have many procedures available to audit, whether you are performing a process audit or system audit.

Augmenting the level 3 procedures are the details for the specific task. These level 4 documents are also considered to be performance standards. Included in the level 4 details are documents such as drawings, purchase orders, product specifications, and inspection plans.

These four levels of documents all have one thing in common: They provide direction on an activity to be accomplished. They are the first element in the P-D-C-A cycle. So a *document* can be considered to be a written description of an action to be accomplished. On the other hand, a *record* is always generated after the event. A record is a written description of an action that has been accomplished. Auditors use documents as their performance standards. Records are used as a form of evidence that the action has been accomplished in accordance with the documented instructions.

In order to provide assurances to your customers, you must examine more than one level of performance standards. The larger, system audits will examine the top part of the pyramid (levels 1–3). The smaller, process audits will examine the bottom part of the pyramid (levels 2–4). If you just examine conformance to a single procedure, you are doing a shallow and ineffective audit.

These performance standards represent the promises made by the audited party. In the overall model of auditing, they represent one of two inputs to the auditing process. They are the controls. Their use in auditing is not optional.

This leads us to the third of five basic *Rules* for quality audits:

3. Measurements are taken against defined standards.

In order to perform an audit, it seems reasonable that you must be aware of the various performance standards to be examined. Locate them. Ask for them. You will need to list them in the Audit Plan (discussion following). You will also need to study them before you can start the fieldwork.

Initial Contact

At this point, you need to make initial contact with those about to be audited. Custom, as well as common courtesy, requires you to let the auditee know what's planned. You also need to discover what level 3 and 4 documents are available. For the internal system audit, this initial contact should be face-to-face between you, the team leader, and someone in the group to be audited. If you can't do this in person, often the case for external audits, then use the telephone. Other, more distant forms of communication, such as voice mail or computer mail, are discouraged.

"But," you might say, "my supplier will not send me the manuals, much less any procedures." This attitude comes from the old style of auditing, where the objective was to find fault and assign blame. Your supplier has probably been hurt by previous auditors, who hit him over the head with his own manual. The natural reaction to such pain is to remove the source of that pain—the manual! You should explain that your purpose is to establish confidence. You need those documents to do your job. If proprietary material is contained in the documents needed, ask that it be removed before you see it. These hostile attitudes will not vanish overnight, but they will change over time.

Administrative details should also be explored for the second-party audit. These details might include security badges, proprietary agreements, suggested hotels, and other travel details. Mutually acceptable dates for the audit should be established so that the right people will be available during the audit period. Little good will result from an audit of a program that was scheduled when most of the participants were attending an important topical conference in Miami. A good rule here is to be firm but flexible.

Initial contact for the smaller, process audits is normally done through publication of the quarterly audit plan, discussed later in this chapter. The folks already know that audits will be performed. They just don't know exactly when. You may show up on the first shift or the third shift, but you will show up. Of course, if you need to find some level 3 or 4 documents, then go to the shift supervisor or group leader and ask for them.

After all the discussions with your client/team members and initial contact with the auditee, you should have a fairly decent knowledge of the various level 1, 2, 3, and 4 performance standards to be used for the audit. Make a list of them.

Understand the Process

You cannot perform an audit successfully (that is, improve performance) unless you have a technical understanding of the processes you will be auditing. By possessing this technical understanding, you will be able to navigate through the processes and ask intelligent questions. However, a caution is in order. Be careful if your team members are *experts* in the field to be audited. Although well meaning, such experts sometimes forget they are auditing and become consultants. This is a violation of basic rule number two (vested interest) and basic rule number three (audit against predefined standards).

Whether you are about to perform a small, process audit or a large, system audit, you must know the basic process steps and the areas or groups involved in those steps. The best way to become knowledgeable in the process is to flowchart the process. This is one of the *seven basic tools* and will be used often in auditing.[2] Know how to flowchart a process!

Once you have placed a visual diagram of the process(es) on paper, you are now in possession of the following knowledge:

- Who does the job?
- What is the job?
- Where is the job done?
- When is the job done?
- Why is the job done?
- How is the job done?

These six words (who, what, where, when, why, how) will be used many times in the audit.

Audit Plan

Now is the time to write down all of the information you have gathered for this upcoming audit. The term used for this written description of the various elements of the upcoming audit is *audit plan*. An audit plan is not the same as an audit schedule. The former tells us what will be covered in a particular audit, or sequence of audits. The latter tells us what audits will be performed within a certain block of time.

The audit plan should be written on one sheet of paper. It should contain the following items:

> Audit Title and Number
>
> Auditee
>
> Purpose
>
> Scope
>
> Performance Standards
>
> Organizations Affected
>
> Any Interfaces
>
> Team Members
>
> Overall Schedule
>
> Review and Approval

The audit plan for a system audit should be specific to that audit. To make things easier, put your first audit plan into the computer. The next time an audit is performed, you can load that earlier file and just change the affected information. All the formatting remains the same. See Figure 2.3 for an example of a system audit plan.

The audit plan for a process audit should cover a series of process audits. This is normally a quarter's worth of audits. All of the above information is placed in the process audit plan, but it covers more than one audit. The schedule would indicate frequency (for example, weekly, first Monday of each month, every other shift) rather than a specific day and time. See Figure 2.4 for an example of a process audit plan.

Audit Plan #AQA 94-06
Corrective Action—Adhesives

Purpose
    To determine whether the department-level procedures for corrective action conform to
    company and ISO 9001 requirements. To determine whether these procedures are
    effective as they apply to the production of ceramic adhesives compounds.

Scope of Audit
    The audit will examine activities associated with ceramic adhesive production since
    January 1994.

Activities to be Audited
    Research and engineering
    Quality control
    Procurement
    Production—ceramic adhesives

Applicable Documents
    ANSI/ASQC Q91-1987
    Acme Adhesives Quality Program Plan
    Acme Adhesives Quality Manual, Section 7
    Acme Process Assurance Procedure, No. 29
    Acme Production Dept. Quality Manual, Section 7

Audit Team Members
    James Red (lead), Susan Black, Lisa Blue, M. Joe Green

Schedule
    Preaudit Meeting   9 A.M.   Oct. 4, 1994
    Audit   Oct. 4–5, 1994
    Postaudit Meeting   4 P.M.   Oct. 5, 1994

Interfaces
    None

Audit Plan Approval: _____ Date: _____
                     Leslie Stewart, Manager
                     Quality Audit Group

Figure 2.3. Example plan for a system audit.

Audit Plan #SAF 94-03
Fire Extinguisher Maintenance

Purpose
　　To determine if fire extinguishers throughout the company are being maintained in a
　　constant state of readiness.

Scope of Audit
　　The audit will examine only portable, handheld extinguishers of 20 lb charge and less.

Activities to be Audited
　　All functional departments within the plant perimeter. All work areas will be included.

Applicable Documents
　　NFPA Std 329—General Requirements for Industrial Fire Protection
　　Acme Adhesives Policy 12—Fire Protection
　　Safety Manual—Chapters 2, 3, and 10
　　Manufacturer's Technical Manuals

Auditor
　　Rebecca Hoffmann

Schedule
　　Jan–Mar 1995: One audit per week, such that all department work areas are examined
　　by the end of March.

Interfaces
　　Guardian Services Insurance local representative.

Audit Plan Approval: _____ Date: _____
　　　　　　　　　　　　Howard Grand, Manager
　　　　　　　　　　　　Plant Maintenance

Figure 2.4. Example plan for a process audit.

Formal Notification

After the audit plan has been prepared, formal notification to the auditee is now in order. This is step number seven in the preparation process. Notification for the small process audit was done when the quarterly audit plan was distributed to affected staff. You need not go out of your way to notify the auditees further. They know you will be coming.

The larger, system audit needs a separate notification each time. For an internal audit notification is done by a memo. For an external audit it is done by a letter. Since you want your audit to address management issues, the notification letter or memo should be addressed to the senior person in charge of the area to be audited. For internal audits this is probably the department manager or area superintendent. For an external audit this is probably the plant manager or president.

Even though you prepared it, the notification letter or memo should be signed by the client, not you. This is an effective way to give your client ownership of the audit and keeps them actively involved in the whole process. Because an external audit involves contractual matters, the letter should be signed by the buyer or purchasing agent.

Standard practice should be to deliver this formal notice at least 30 days before the actual field visit. This forces you to become better prepared and it also gives them time to get ready. Thus, the notification for process audits is distributed four times a year; a month prior to the beginning of each quarter. Each system audit should have a separate notification letter or memo.

Evaluate Performance Standards

As discussed earlier, management audits evaluate the adequacy of controls as well as compliance with those controls. Although you don't challenge the adequacy of level 1 (policy) documents, you cannot assume that the lower level 2, 3, and 4 documents are going to totally and effectively implement those policies. Because you can perform this evaluation of lower-tier documents to higher-tier standards at your desk, before the fieldwork starts, we call this a *desk audit*. It is step number eight in the preparation process. The desk audit serves two purposes.

1. Determine whether lower-level documents adequately respond to identified requirements of their higher-level performance standards.

2. Obtain a better understanding of the program activity so that the performance phase of the audit can be completed in an efficient and effective manner.

In performing the desk audit you should start from the highest-level document you have. (You obtained copies of these policies, standards, codes, manuals, procedures, and so on, earlier for the flowchart process in step six.) Break the document down into the basic control elements, such as identify important processes, obtain bids from preapproved sources, approve all assembly instructions prior to use, or schedule internal audits. Note that these are all action statements; they contain a verb and an object for that verb.

As you progress through the document, make a list of all these action statements. If you place them in a column down the left side of a page (or computer screen), it will be easier to record additional data to the right of each action statement. Now pick up the lower-level document and attempt to find the location, by paragraph number, where the action statement is addressed. Not all higher-level action statements need be addressed in a single lower-level document. In fact, they will probably be scattered among many lower-level documents. If you find the control item (action statement) addressed, write down the document and paragraph where you found it next to that control item. If, after searching all your sources, you cannot find a control addressed, make a note of it next to that control item. If the procedure seems vague in its application of the control requirement, then mark your list accordingly; you will need to examine these areas in greater detail later in the fieldwork. Also, your study will identify specific records, forms, or reports that are used to implement the required action. These should also be noted on your list, along with identification of the person or place where those records should be available.

When you are finished with all level 1 documents, go to the level 2 documents and make another list of control items from that level. Attempt to find these new controls in documents further down the line. All of this effort will lead to a much greater understanding of the way various activities are designed to work. When finished, you now have a cross reference of the controls to be examined and the document locations of each. This will be of great value in the later writing of checklists.

Checklists

Recall from the overall model of auditing presented earlier that there are two inputs to the process of auditing: controls (what should be) and data (what is). In order to gather this data, you need to know what it is. Just as you should prepare a list of groceries to buy before you go to the super-market, you should prepare a list of data to gather before you gather it. The purpose of a checklist is to gather data.

This leads us to the fourth of five basic *Rules* for quality audits:

4. Conclusions are based on fact.

The team will be expected to examine all of the selected control areas iden-tified from the various performance standards chosen for your audit. Additionally, a method is needed for organizing all of the information gathered during the course of the audit. An effective audit checklist will meet both of these needs. A checklist is one of the distinguishing differ-ences between an audit and other, less formal, methods of performance monitoring. The checklist serves as a guide to each member of the audit team, in order to assure that the full scope of the audit is adequately cov-ered. It also provides a place for recording the facts gathered during the fieldwork. A written checklist, prepared before the field visit, is required.

Forms of Data

As you prepare your audit checklist, you should be aware of the five types of data to be gathered in the fieldwork (Figure 2.5). An analogy might be the picking of flowers in order to make a nice flower arrangement. You go out into the field of flowers (the auditee's work area) and pick some flowers (gather data). You place these flowers (data) into your basket (checklist). Then you take your basket of flowers inside to make a nice arrangement (audit report). No flowers—no flower arrangement. No data—no audit report. There are five kinds of flowers.

1. Physical properties

2. Information from your senses

3. Documents and records

4. Interviews

5. Patterns

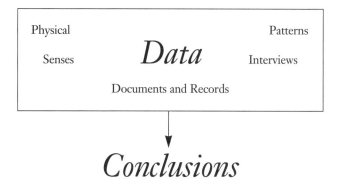

Figure 2.5. Data-driven decisions.

The official term used for these various types of data is *objective evidence.* The ISO 10011 quality systems auditing standard refers to a statement based on data as an *observation.*

Physical Properties

This is the measurement, inspection, or count of tangible items. Examples of physical properties include the following:

- Markings on floppy disks
- Sizes of file folders
- The color of a wall
- The layout of a work area

Make sure, however, that you are qualified to measure something before you report it as a fact. Physical properties are regarded as one of the most reliable types of audit evidence. They represent reality. Your audience will have little difficulty relating to these tangible things when they are presented in the final report.

Information from Your Senses

Throughout an audit, there are many opportunities to use your sight, hearing, touch, and smell to evaluate a wide range of situations. By watching an action being performed, you can determine how the system is actually being implemented. Occasionally, you might be able to smell or hear something, but normally your eyes will be the primary means of input. Often this is accomplished by asking the operator to demonstrate a particular action to you. Have the operator conduct a database search and watch the action. See how a form is actually completed by following the other party around as they complete the various steps. As you watch, you are continually taking notes of the specific actions and items being accomplished. You are also asking questions to test the performer's knowledge of the procedure steps. By using your senses (mostly your eyes), you base your report on actual activities being performed. The report is more realistic than if you had limited yourself to just the paperwork.

Documents and Records

Documents are used to specify an action, while records are used to substantiate that something was performed and that it met requirements. Most important transactions and processes should be supported by a document. Often, records will be generated as a result of these controlled actions. So there is a large volume of this type of evidence available to you. Records are the most frequently used source of information, but are also the most frequently abused. You must remember that all activities are not, and should not be, recorded on a piece of paper just to make the auditor's job easier. If it is not recorded, look for evidence elsewhere.

Interviews

This is the process of obtaining information from another person in response to your questions. The methods used for conducting interviews will be discussed in the next chapter.

Patterns

Comparisons and relationships among data points may be used as a means of isolating or highlighting certain activities. You may compare the way two groups perform the same task. Another example of this type of evidence would be to conduct a trend analysis on such things as the number of field support calls per month over the past year to determine whether the rate for a certain code version is increasing or decreasing. (This also allows you to determine if the code change made things better or worse.) Other examples of patterns include trend analysis (increasing or decreasing), percentages, and ratios. Actually, patterns originate from one or more of the above four forms of data.

Contents of the Checklist

There are certain criteria that any audit checklist should include, regardless of the audit subject or scope. Obviously, the checklist must first provide for clear identification of the specific audit topic or subject to which it applies, the organization(s) to be audited, and the audit dates. A unique reference number may be assigned to your audit and this, too, will be identified in the heading information of the checklist.

Remember, the main function of the checklist is to gather data. This is done by listing the specific points to be examined. The format by which this is accomplished will vary from office to office. Some choose to list the questions in a column down the left side of the page. This is followed by a center column for checking *yes/no* or *sat/unsat*, and another column on the right side for recording the objective evidence examined for that question. Others choose to simply list the questions on the page with an inch or two of white space between questions for recording notes and reference to objective evidence. Any workable format is acceptable.

Each checklist question should address one piece of information. If you try to include many facts in one question, you will wind up confused and probably miss some of those reminders when you get to the field.

Checklist questions are not the open-ended questions to be discussed in the field; rather, they are the individual facts you will need to form conclusions. They must be precise. They must be measurable. They must be facts. To better accomplish this, try to phrase your checklist questions in *yes* or *no* form. This makes your questions binary, as opposed to the analog-type questions you will ask in the interview.

The questions should also reference the specific section of the standard that established a particular requirement. These cross-references not only provide you with a handy reply to the question, Where did that requirement come from? but they also force precision in the development of the checklist in the first place. This keeps you away from the temptation to make up the rules.

One approach often used for the development of checklist questions is to separate each requirement paragraph of a particular standard into smaller, manageable bits, then to rephrase those requirements in the form of questions needing a *yes* or *no* answer. As stated before, these are intended as questions for you to answer after review of the procedures, completion of interviews, and examination of evidence. In other words, you must determine whether the group being reviewed does or does not meet requirements.

When preparing your checklist questions, you must be careful not to change the essential requirements of the standard by careless use of similar words, as you have no authority for rewording a requirement to reflect your own bias or preferred way of accomplishing a task.

Collection Plan

It is also necessary to include a plan for the collection of specific evidence needed to answer certain checklist questions. What do you wish to look at? How many items do you want to sample? What are the criteria you will use to judge acceptability? These are the types of questions that should be addressed in the checklist. Naturally, you won't know all of the places to look prior to the audit, but you should be aware of some (Figure 2.6).

The collection plan should provide you with space for recording the results of your examinations, including an identification of those people you talked with. As mentioned previously, some people prefer columns for entering data and interview results, while others prefer white space between individual questions. A matrix arrangement works especially well for collection plans. You should use the format that works best for you, as these become your notes and the success of the audit may depend upon how well you can reconstruct an interview or record review.

Here are the 11 steps to be taken in building a checklist.

1. Pull out your flowchart of the process(es) to be audited.

2. Choose the first action step.

3. Develop yes/no questions dealing with *methods* affectors of that action.

4. Develop yes/no questions dealing with *material* affectors of that action.

5. Develop yes/no questions dealing with *machinery* affectors of that action.

6. Develop yes/no questions dealing with *manpower* affectors of that action.

7. Develop yes/no questions dealing with *measurement* affectors of that action.

Collection Plan Audit #INS 94-10						
Select six carpet samples from the last two production shifts:	**1**	**2**	**3**	**4**	**5**	**6**
1. Record the type of carpet						
2. Record the color						
3. Record the production run number						
4. Was the sample at least 10 cm × 10 cm in size? (SIM 3.2, ¶ 5.1)						
5. Was the run number recorded on the QC inspection sheet? (SIM 3.2, ¶ 5.7)						
6. Was the color test device calibrated within 48 hours of use? (Tech Man 6-1)						
7. Were inspection results available prior to release of the production run? (BMM 4, ¶ 13)						
8. Were anomalies reported to the shift supervisor within 1 hour? (BMM 4, ¶ 13)						

Figure 2.6. Example collection plan.

8. Develop yes/no questions dealing with *environment* affectors of that action.

9. Go to the next action step in the process.

10. Develop the *methods, material, machinery, manpower, measurement,* and *environment* questions for that step.

11. Continue to work your way through the flowchart in this manner.

Standard Checklists

Some organizations like to use *canned* checklists, which, once prepared and approved, are used for all subsequent audits. By themselves, these standard checklists do not reflect how a particular department, factory, or branch office assigns responsibilities and authority. They fail to identify special features of a particular program that may be crucial to success. They only address some of the performance criteria, usually only the top level. Additionally, they allow the audit to proceed without really adequate preparation and thought; you do not have to think as hard. The use of standard checklists by themselves is not recommended. However, previous checklists can provide you with a bank of potential questions for recycling. With the advent of personal computers, along with word processing software, use of these banks of questions can significantly reduce checklist preparation time.

On the other hand, standard checklists can be used as a starting point for your inquiries. You might use it as a framework. Lower level performance standards, such as manuals, procedures, and run plans, should be used to complete the checklist. Appendix D is presented in this spirit.

For the individual process audit, a common set of questions to be explored for each area is appropriate. These questions are used each time the process audit is performed, until the campaign is finished. Then a new set of questions is prepared for the next process audit.

Checklist Assignments

It is the responsibility of each audit team member to prepare specific checklist questions appropriate to their assigned portion of the job. For example, one individual might be assigned to examine document control, another to control of the computer source code library, and a third to calibration of test instruments. Each individual would identify specific requirements applicable to the assigned area and enter them onto a checklist.

When finished with the checklist development, each team member should submit his or her portion to peer review. This serves as a check of thoroughness, proper logic construction, and absence of bias. Any qualified reviewer will do. This may be the team leader, another team member, or your group manager. The purpose of this review should not be to approve your checklist, but rather to subject it to a critical examination of content. Better checklists and thus better audits will result from this practice. Once done, the review should be recorded somewhere so that you may take credit for it. Usually, a signature and date at the bottom of the first page of the checklist is satisfactory.

History

In developing checklists and preparing for the audit, it helps to know the history of the area under review and how successful its implementation has been. You or someone else may have performed a previous audit in this or a similar area. If this is the case, you should review records of prior audits and identify from the records any specific area likely to have continuing or repeat problems. If the prior audit revealed any noncompliance to requirements, you should determine the current status of actions that were taken to resolve the noncompliance. The previous audit team leader may have closed out these items based on information that specific corrective actions were implemented. The new audit team should verify that these actions have remained in effect, and that they have been effective in preventing recurrence of the problem or noncompliance. Previous nonconformance reports and program assessment reports may also prove to be useful in identifying areas to explore.

In your review of past audits of this program, you also want to note the strengths that were previously identified. One of the objectives of your audit should be to verify that these strengths have not eroded through changes in personnel, equipment, office reorganization, or many other reasons.

For external, supplier audits, this may also be a good time to discuss the supplier's performance with various users. They may have particular areas of interest that merit examination by your audit team. Also, these users are the ones that stand to gain the most from the supplier's improved performance, which is the goal of a second-party audit.

Add this review information to the audit checklist. This is another reason to avoid the use of canned checklists; they cannot be revised to account for additional information, as would come from your review of the supplier's history. The checklist is a constantly evolving document that is modified right up to the point of preparing the audit report.

Summary

The following are the products of the preparation phase:

- An audit plan
- An audit checklist
- Logistical arrangements completed
- An initial evaluation of the control methods
- A plan for the collecting of facts

The audit plan will identify the organization to be audited, the subject or purpose of the audit and its scope, the activities to be reviewed, members of the audit team, and the documents (performance standards) applicable to the audit.

The audit checklist will identify the various items intended to be examined and the reference location for each requirement. It will show the various facts you need to obtain during the audit. The checklist will contain space for recording both bad facts and good facts, along with space to record comments and notes regarding certain conclusions.

The auditee has been informed of the audit—its purpose, scope, and authority. Mutually agreeable dates have been established for the audit and a rough audit schedule has been developed. Copies of the various control documents and organization charts have been obtained, along with additional procedures and instructions applicable to the audit. Travel arrangements, including hotel reservations, have also been made.

From the review of the auditee's control methods (desk audit) and discussions with the users, you have identified areas of probable strengths and weaknesses in the activity to be evaluated. You have also prepared a plan for collecting evidence. With the audit plan and checklist in hand, and with the necessary arrangements made, you are well on your way.

Notes

1. *ISO 10011-1:1990, Guidelines for Quality Systems Audits.* (Geneva: International Standards Organization, 1990): 3.

2. The Seven Basic Tools include flowcharts, control charts, cause-and-effect diagrams, histograms, check sheets, Pareto charts, and scatter diagrams. See the June through December 1990 issues of *Quality Progress* magazine for more details on these tools.

Chapter 3

Performance

The performance phase of an audit is often called the fieldwork. It is the data-gathering portion of the audit and covers the time period from arrival at the audit location up to, but not including, the exit meeting. It consists of the following activities:

- Meeting with the auditee
- Understanding the process and system controls
- Verifying these controls work
- Communicating among team members
- Communicating with the auditee

Each of these activities will be explored in greater detail so that you gain a better understanding of the skills and mechanics needed.

Opening Meeting

All audits must have some sort of opening meeting. This starts the data-gathering phase of the audit. The opening meeting, sometimes called an entrance meeting, is held soon after your arrival at the audit site. You should have your entire team at the meeting, so that they may be introduced. The audit team leader should take charge of the meeting and keep it brief. Most opening meetings can be completed in 15 minutes, if you know what you are doing and are adequately prepared. Prepare an agenda for the meeting and pass out copies before starting. Elaborate presentations by the auditee only waste time. They are not needed. Remember, the more time spent watching a show, the less time you have for observing, checking, and questioning.

For the system audit it would be ideal to meet with the manager of the area to be audited. If an assistant shows up, that is fine. If you only get a records clerk for the opening meeting, you should tactfully request someone from management. The smaller, process audit is much less formal. Normally, a simple, two-minute meeting between you, the auditor, and the shift supervisor is sufficient.

Several things should be accomplished in the opening meeting. First, the purpose and scope of the audit should be restated. The managers present may have only vague notions of what to expect, especially if this is their first audit experience. Usually, however, the group has been examined before and will have some idea of what to expect. The audit team leader should set the tone of the meeting by stating the purpose and scope in a clear and diplomatic fashion. Even though this information has already been published in the notification letter, it may not have been received (or understood) by those present. The audit team and their counterparts should also trade introductions, sometimes with a brief description of backgrounds and/or positions. This is a good time to present your credentials.

You can form important judgments during the opening meeting. Are they relaxed or anxious, open or defensive? What seems to be the style of the group? Is the director alone and trying to dominate the meeting? Is the staff in attendance and do they participate? These observations will prove valuable in understanding people's reactions during interviews. They will also help when developing the tone of the report. You must impress upon those in attendance that you know what they do. Reinforce the study that was done during the preparation phase by asking specific questions about the group's activities.

You might want to solicit areas of interest from those at the meeting. Often, the response might be a desire on their part for you to examine a newly revised area, such as data reduction or records handling. They may also wish to know how they stack up against other organizations performing similar tasks.

Conversely, you may have areas of particular concern for this audit. If your research during the preparation phase has indicated a potential weak area, it should be mentioned. This will help your counterparts to prepare for your intense examination of that area of interest.

If not already accomplished before the opening meeting, the audit checklists should be presented to the auditee now. It is a good idea for the team leader to have at least four copies available—one to give to the senior auditee representative as a display of respect, two to keep for the fieldwork, and another for reproducing right after the meeting.

The most important part of the entrance meeting is to set the detailed schedule. It affects all the effort to come and allows the audit to proceed efficiently. A good way to accomplish this is to develop a matrix of team members and areas, with dates and times to be filled in at the opening meeting. By discussing the information needs with your counterparts, you may be able to designate blocks of time for specified individuals. This accomplishes four important things.

1. It forces the audit process along.

2. It provides for good time management by those being audited.

3. It encourages a constant application of your resources over the entire audit.

4. It sends a strong message of cooperation to those about to be audited (Figure 3.1).

Such things as conference rooms, telephone access, safety considerations, hours of operation, and lunchroom facilities can also be discussed. Often, in the larger, system audit, a guide or *shadow* from the auditee organization will be assigned to assist you and your team. The use of a guide is encouraged. This person is there to point you in the right direction and offer advice on who is responsible for a particular activity. They must not be allowed to provide you with all the answers, however. Your guide will usually take notes on what you are asking and examining. This is fine and contributes to the free exchange of information between auditor and auditee.

Gather the Facts

The data-gathering process normally takes most of the time and effort in the performance phase of the audit. Recall from earlier discussions that the job of the auditor is to gather facts, compare these facts to requirements,

	D. Arter	S. Clark
Mon A.M.	Entrance meeting	Entrance meeting
Mon P.M.	Project B383	Project B455
Tue A.M.	Training	Project B455
Tue P.M.	Work order 250270	Work order 251250
Wed A.M.	Work order 250270	Drawing control
Wed P.M.	Records	Inspection
Project B383	John Burkhart	HQ 5th floor
Project B455	Tom Campbell	HQ 4th floor
Work orders	Robert Rubel	Bldg 210
Administration	Dennis Sandmeier	Bldg 19

Figure 3.1. Detailed audit schedule.

and report the results to management. The checklist, prepared earlier, is the repository of these facts. It is a place to record the five types of data.

1. Physical properties

2. Information from your senses

3. Documents and records

4. Interviews

5. Patterns

Also remember that the fundamental questions to be answered by an audit are the following:

- Whether controls exist and are adequate
- Whether controls are being implemented
- Whether controls really work

Preparing for the audit will begin to answer the first of these questions, but you need tangible proof that your conclusions, both positive and negative, are credible. The best way to obtain this proof is by examination of the product, which is the output of the organization you are auditing.

In a factory the product is usually readily identifiable—valves, canned peas, relays, tires, and doors. But the product of a service group is harder to define. Try to come up with something tangible. For example, the product of a purchasing group might be the finished purchase order. The product of a human resources group might be an offer of employment and subsequent employment contract. The product of a government agency might be a regulatory decision. Regardless of the activity being audited, you must find a way to tie your conclusions back to something tangible. The easiest way to accomplish this tie is through the technique of tracing.

Tracing

Tracing is a common means of collecting objective evidence (facts) during an audit. It can involve almost every facet of the system being examined and will result in a well-defined picture of actual practices. To trace means to follow the progress of something as it is processed. The item being traced may be tangible (for example, a popsicle) or intangible (for example, information). The way to start is to pull out the flowchart of the activity, which you prepared in step six of the preparation phase. This can be used as a road map for your tracing activities.

The mechanics of tracing are relatively simple.

- Start either at the beginning, middle, or the end of the process.

- Choose an action, such as painting a wall.

- Gather information on the six process affectors (methods, machinery, material, manpower, measurement, and environment) for that action. Be sure to record this information on your checklist. Write down what you see, who you talk to, where you are, when the action was done, why the action is accomplished, and how it is accomplished. These become your facts for later use.

- Follow the path of the transaction backward or forward through the process.

It is usually more meaningful to trace a product backward through the process. Start with distribution, then proceed to the lab, then go to final blending, then go to solvent extraction, and so on. By tracing backward, you are examining product actually being shipped. This stuff is going to the customer. Your conclusions will represent reality, not some *what if* situation.

Data collection by tracing rests upon the assumption that the path taken fairly represents the actual functioning of the process. Therefore, you must be careful while being led through the maze by your guide.

Match what you are seeing with what you studied in the preparation phase. If significant differences arise, ask why.

Interviews

This is the process of obtaining information from another person in response to your questions. It is the most important form of data you can gather in auditing. It is also very difficult to do. At first you will be very nervous. This is not something most folks come by naturally. It has to be practiced.

Although considerable information is obtained through an interview, it cannot usually be regarded as conclusive because of communication barriers we erect between one another. You may not have heard the reply; they may not have heard the question. Additionally, the other party may not have the big picture as you do. When someone tells you something, it is not yet a fact. It is a pseudofact. Only after that statement has been corroborated, can you use what you heard as a fact.

There are three ways to corroborate the information received in an interview.

1. Another person says the same thing. Of course, they need not use the exact same words, but the message (information) is the same as that heard earlier. To have maximum value, try to choose someone from another group or management level to corroborate the first story.

2. Another member of your team hears the same thing. The information can come from the same person you spoke to earlier or another person. Regardless of the second source, another set of ears has received the *same* message, so the likelihood of a miscommunication is less.

3. An item, document, or record verifies the action. You've heard the explanation and then read a procedure stating the action as explained. Or perhaps you see a completed form with the information just described. Note that this is but one of the three forms of corroboration. It is an important form, but not the only way to remove communication barriers.

None of these methods will show that the action is correct, but they will allow you to place faith in the information just received. The methods described may be right or they may not be right, but they are now fact. If you get conflicting stories, then you do not have a fact. If you get ten versions of an action from twelve people, the fact is, "Nobody knows the correct method." You must get enough sources saying the same thing to allow you to state, "Yup. I now know the truth."

Interview Technique

A good auditor possesses skill, training, and personal attitudes of a special nature. Part of this magical quality is the ability to conduct useful interviews. (Recall from earlier discussion that an interview is one of the five forms of data and that data are required in order to write a report.)

The interview process can be broken down into six steps.[1]

1. Put the person at ease.

2. Explain your purpose.

3. Find out what they are doing.

4. Analyze what they are doing.

5. Make a tentative conclusion.

6. Explain your next step.

In each of these steps, you must deal with the human person. Remember, they possess the information you need for success!

1. Put them at ease.

Consider yourself as a guest in their home and show the respect you would naturally give to your host. Your purpose here is to give that other person an opportunity to size you up and to lower the natural sense of anxiety. This step may range from a simple introduction and handshake to discussions about the parking lot or weather. Often, the person being interviewed is threatened by your presence and may even perceive their job to be in jeopardy if *wrong* answers are given. Unless these barriers are removed, little information will be obtained. This introduction period should last about a minute.

2. Explain your purpose.

The natural first reaction to your presence might be, "Why me?" You must address that concern immediately. What information do you want? Why are you asking all these questions? Most people will express a desire to share information once they know why you want it. In this way it makes them feel important. A useful technique here is to show the other person a copy of your blank checklist. Right away, they can see the questions, understand the data you need, and make a decision as to whether they have that information. Of course, ask for your checklist back at the end of the discussion, so that you may use it again.

It is in this early stage of the interview process that a demonstration of competence is important. You should be aware of the effect your appearance has on others and dress in a smart, businesslike manner. More important, however, is the impression created by being well organized and exhibiting a knowledge of the subject matter. You need not be an expert in the processes, but you should at least be aware of the commonly used terms and associated methods. Use words they understand, without talking up or down to them. Be careful, however, to refrain from discussing explicit controls or practices that you have seen elsewhere. Such showing off will only damage your usefulness. Of course, you should never discuss business-sensitive matters with unauthorized people.

3. Find out what they are doing.

During your preparation for the audit, you should have examined the level 1–4 documents affecting this area. You have already identified areas to explore. You now continue the investigation process by asking open-ended questions: "How does the Ogden Service Center use this information?" "What is your first action upon receipt of a data input form?" "What are the common actions or events that start this program going?" Use questions that begin with who, what, where, when, why, and how.[2] By avoiding questions which give *yes* or *no* answers, you will get much more information. If the answers are incomplete, try, "And then what happens?"

Remember that the questions you ask here are not the same as those that appear on your checklist. These are the exploratory questions designed to get you the data. One of these open-ended questions will probably get you several answers for your checklist.

You should also avoid statements such as "I understand you keep the Disk Inventory Sheet." In legal circles this is called a *leading question* and is designed to elicit a specific response. The way you phrase the question leads the respondent to give you the answer they think you are expecting.

During this part of the interview process, it is necessary to get that other person to show you the forms, printouts, and memos being discussed. Remember, you need facts for your conclusions. This not only helps you to understand the control process, it also contributes to the examination by providing concrete examples of the verbal explanations. It also directs some of the natural tension toward an inanimate piece of paper.

You have two ears and one mouth, so you should probably listen twice as long as you talk! This is certainly not the time to lecture the other person or brag about your accomplishments. If your question produces a satisfactory answer, make a notation on your checklist and proceed to the next question. The necessary pause periods while you write should be as brief as possible. You should always strive to reduce tensions; silence is usually uncomfortable. One technique that is often quite effective is to *write out loud* as you place information on your checklist. Also remember that this is not a trial.

You now have a bunch of marks and notes on your checklist. You have gathered a lot of information, but you are not finished with the interview yet! Some important (and often forgotten) steps follow.

4. Analyze what they are doing.

Once you have heard the words, you must analyze what those words mean. If you are familiar with the control process being discussed, your job here becomes somewhat easier. When there is a logical break in the questioning, repeat the answers back, using different words, to improve the chance that you understand. "Let me see if I have that straight; first you receive the item and note its properties and then . . . ." Such thinking out loud, also known as paraphrasing, forces you to put the facts in perspective and in some sort of logical arrangement. Draw boxes and flowcharts on your checklist page notes. Underline important issues. Draw stars.

Sometimes you will receive an answer that is incomplete or clearly at variance with the written requirements. Attempt to resolve the issue by looking for areas of agreement and defer the area of disagreement for later. Give the other person the opportunity to save face—the omission or lack of control may not have been important after all, or it may have been an inadvertent error. It is useful to stress supporting or contributing statements and assure yourself that you are not nitpicking.

This step may be the most difficult for those just learning audit methods. Not only do you have to actively listen to the words, but you also have to match the incoming data with your understanding of the requirements. At the same time, you are placing words on your checklist and developing words for the next question. It's hard!

5. Make a tentative conclusion.
It is now time to state your conclusions. This concept of no secrets is sometimes hard to practice; we don't want to tell someone that they are doing something wrong. This is why annual performance reports are often deferred or meaningless. But you are obligated to tell the interviewee what you think. Your final report will benefit as well.

If your initial analysis indicates that all is well, it is appropriate to say, "The system as I understand it appears to be as follows . . . , and that meets the requirements of . . . ." Let that other person know that he or she is doing something good. They will continue to perform well with such recognition by an outsider.

If there is a deficiency, give them an opportunity to produce additional factual evidence to show that you have made an error. The discussion should be unemotional and professional. Do not convey glee at having found a deficiency or anger at what seems to be an evasive answer. Remember that you will have the last word in the report. You know it and they know it. A problem cannot be solved by taking a stand or playing win/lose. If doubt remains at the end of the discussion, then say so. Do not say, "You haven't convinced me of . . .;" rather say, "There still seems to me to be an opening . . .; perhaps I'll understand it better when I review the data."

By practicing this philosophy of no secrets, any errors you may have made will be corrected early in this interview phase rather than at a formal closing meeting or after the report is issued. There is a strong desire on the part of that other person to make your problem disappear. The overwhelming desire is to turn that tentative conclusion around. In doing so that person must give you additional facts. The only way that can occur is for you to be provided with more data. You have just turned that other person into an auditor! You have, in effect, leveraged your audit. If the audit is successful and your problem is resolved, that other person wins. If it is unsuccessful, eventually the other person will be convinced that a problem exists. The auditor wins again, in that the problem can now be corrected. Additionally, you have provided vital feedback to the employee; good performance will continue and poor performance will be corrected. Everyone wins!

6. Explain your next step.

The final step of the interview process is to conclude the discussions and let that other person know what's next. If you feel that you have about all the information you can get, then state, "Thank you for your help. I don't believe we'll need to get back with you again." Whew! The person can now go back to work and once more be a productive employee. If all your questions have not been answered, you may wish to make another appointment. If you intend to check out additional records as a result of the interview, then this, too, should be stated. It is important to remember that people want to know the following:

- How they did in the interview
- Whether they are finished

The keys to a good interview are rigorous preparation, and a genuine desire to know and understand the other person's viewpoint. You must remember that these are other human beings and not printed circuits with whom you are dealing. They have the advantage of having a valuable commodity (information) that you desire. If you act like a guest in their home and stick to the principle of no secrets, your interview will be a success.

Perceptions

Most of us recognize that the world as we see it is not necessarily as it really is. A good job to one of us may be a sloppy job to another. Often, we are presented with the same set of facts as someone else. Our perception of these facts and resulting conclusions will be different depending upon our individual needs and viewpoints. People, including auditors, see things differently (Figure 3.2). You may have developed considerable bias over time. You may have familiarity with the company way of doing things. Of course, the same thing has happened to those you will be auditing. These different views may be quite honestly and stubbornly held.

You must recognize this situation and attempt to overcome it. Here are some concepts to consider if you wish to persuade your customers that

Figure 3.2. Two people and two animals.

your perception of the facts is better (more useful) than their perception of those same facts.

- Present items and facts that will satisfy the needs of the affected organizations. Make a contribution. Show how the facts affect the product or service.

- Ignore or downplay mildly disturbing things. Don't nitpick. Strive to answer the "So what?" reaction.

- Pay attention to significant things. Chronic or persistent problems and weaknesses, along with trends, will get the attention of your audience.

- Above all, try to relate what you are seeing to accepted business values. The radio station most of us listen to is WII-FM (What's in it for Me). Songs heard over WII-FM include cost, schedule, grievances, overtime, customer complaints, and missed shipments. These are the important driving forces in the lives of your intended audience.

Granted, these concepts have much to do with the report of the audit and the way in which you present your conclusions, but you must be aware of these needs and perceptions during the performance phase in order to gather the proper information. Additionally, you will have many opportunities to present small summaries and conclusions throughout the audit. You should be prepared to address these perception issues from the beginning.

Team Meetings

For the larger, system audit, it is sound practice to leave about 30 minutes prior to lunch and at the end of each day for your team to meet. (Process audits will normally be conducted by one person. You don't need to meet with yourself.) These caucus sessions should be informal and include the following activities:

- Share facts, tentative conclusions, and problems.
- Replan for the next day's activities. This is sort of a repeat of the preparation phase.
- Develop the report.

Sharing facts and tentative conclusions enriches the audit process. Talking over what has been learned during the day's investigation allows for team corroboration of facts and possible areas for deeper investigation. Discussions should also include the perceptions drawn during the interview process. Is there an activity that is done extremely well or very poorly? Does the evidence gathered by each individual team member point to a more general conclusion about the controls used and their implementation? The questions and discussions should bring into sharper focus tentative conclusions for the report. Facts collected during the day should be organized and sorted in order to support these conclusions, both positive and negative. Where pieces of evidence are either insufficient or completely missing, you can then make plans to fill in these gaps.

The result from this sharing could be replanning or redirection of the audit. Keep in mind, however, that you are obligated to stick to the original purpose and scope. Based on information now available, the following issues can be addressed:

- Are the results of the interviews and other data gathering sufficient to reach a conclusion?

- Should there be additional interviews, additional checklist questions, or additional records reviewed? Do you need more data?
- Are there administrative problems to be resolved with the group being audited or your audit team?
- Does the audit seem to be accomplishing its objectives?

Tentative Conclusions

As you conduct interviews and gather data, you will reach conclusions about the performance of the auditee. You should write these down in draft form. They may be either good or bad practices, but they should be considered for the final report. At the team meeting these draft statements may be polished, consolidated with others, or discarded. In any event they are extremely useful for beginning the reporting phase.

Daily Briefings

For the larger, system audit, you can now see that effective team meetings are important to success. Likewise, daily briefings with the auditee will enhance the quality of your system audit. If a goal of improved performance is to be attained, it is important that there be *NO SURPRISES* at all levels. This communication can be strengthened by a short and informal briefing of about 10 minutes at the end of each day with a representative from their group, normally your guide or *shadow*. Topics to be discussed include the following:

- Checklist areas completed
- Checklist areas to be examined (or revisited) tomorrow
- Any areas of concern
- Any problems experienced

If you've uncovered something out of whack, it is certainly not necessary (or desirable) to present polished conclusions yet. Rather, explain to the representative that these are potential problem areas or areas of concern at this stage. You know that as soon as this meeting is finished, the representative will brief his or her manager. They will try to make that problem go away. The auditee organization becomes motivated to help you by providing additional facts to verify or refute your concerns. If you were wrong because of incorrect or insufficient information, the item is prevented from appearing in the final report. If they truly do have a problem, the additional investigating has helped to reinforce the fact. Either way, both parties win.

Onward

The next phase of the audit process is the reporting phase, although you may have noticed that much of the discussion in this chapter has concerned itself with the report. This is because there is no sharp boundary line between the two phases. The report is being proposed, modified, rejected, and rebuilt by the entire team both individually and jointly as the audit progresses. You must keep it in the back of your mind constantly. Starting the report on the first day of data gathering has at least four merits.

1. It helps structure the audit by forcing you to develop hypotheses early.

2. The writing of tentative conclusions forces precision in the process.

3. The problem of sorting, understanding, and reviewing a large mass of material before the exit meeting deadline is reduced.

4. Factual errors, perceptual errors, and other distortions are reduced.

The next chapter contains more detailed discussion on the specific aspects of your report.

Notes

1. Original concept developed by Frank X. Brown, *The Practice and Process of Auditing* (Pittsburgh: Westinghouse Electric Corporation, 1979).

2. "I keep six honest serving men (They taught me all I knew); Their names are What and Why and When and How and Where and Who." from Rudyard Kipling, "The Elephant Child" from *Just-So Stories* (New York: Knopf, 1992).

Chapter 4

Reporting

The Report Is Your Product

The audit report is your final *product*. All of the sights, sounds, smells, observations, scraps of paper, tensions, and anxieties are finally reduced into something for others to read. When everything is closed out, the only evidence of your presence is the report! It is your means of communicating information to others. As such, it should have certain characteristics in order to be successful.

Regardless of the source or purpose, it is generally accepted that reports should have accuracy, conciseness, clarity, timeliness, and tone.[1] The report must be completely factual, in that every statement and reference must be based on one of the five forms of data discussed in the preceding chapter. It must be concise so that superfluous words do not block reception of the message. This goes right to the issue of clarity—the ability to put your thoughts into the mind of the reader. If your report is not issued in a timely fashion, the facts will have been forgotten and other crises will have taken the attention of your audience. Finally, the tone of the report must be courteous and professional; it must sound like the voice of management.

In addition to these traits, which are common to all reports, your report needs to possess the additional characteristics of relevance, consistency, and comparability.[2] Unless your report is relevant to the business needs of your customers, it will be largely ignored. Consistency of reports over the year is desirable to show trends and provide for greater comprehension by the reader. After they are familiar with format and contents, they know where to look for desired information. Finally, reports from a number of auditors should be comparable to allow for maximum efficiency and fairness.

Verifiability

Your reports should be verifiable. The reader may not always be able to verify them personally, since we cannot track down the evidence for every piece of history known. But if you use generally accepted names for things (for example, foot, yard, milling machine, and batch preparation files), there is relatively little danger of your message being misunderstood. When you refer to specific items or locations at the audit site, the perception of verifiability is enhanced. Of course, one of the main purposes of a structured checklist is to record supporting information (facts). However, putting checklist-like detail in the report makes it too cumbersome and unreadable. Additionally, the reader tends to become tangled in the checklist details and may miss the overall message of the report. Your completed checklist should be kept in the office file as backup. It should not be included with the report.

Even though it appears (especially to the new auditor) as if everybody seems to be quarreling with everybody else, we still trust information from others. We ask street directions of total strangers. We follow directions on microwave popcorn packages without being suspicious of the people who wrote those directions. We read books about science, space travel, the history of party dresses, and even fishing, and we assume that the author is trying hard to tell the true story. Most of the time, we are safe in our assumptions. There is an enormous amount of reliable information available. Deliberate misinformation is still more the exception than the rule. The reader wants to believe your report because of basic human desires. With simple, clear, and direct language, you can reinforce those desires.

Inferences

An inference is a statement about the unknown made on the basis of the known. You may infer lack of control over donut size from your examination of the blending and mixing instructions. You may infer lack of actual control from the fact that two out of five, or six out of 24, donuts pulled from the line were too small. In fact, an audit requires that you make inferences such as these. The question is not, "Should you make inferences?" but rather, "Are you aware of the inferences you make?" The technique of gathering and analyzing facts will allow you to present these inferences in an understandable and logical fashion. Anyone may retrace your path and should make the same inference. But since this is unlikely to happen, you must take the approach that a reasonable person, presented with the same facts you have seen, will draw conclusions similar to yours. Their inferences will match yours.

As a practical matter, most people will need more convincing (stronger facts and more of them) if the inference does not support a previously held conviction. This is not surprising. Any student of debate knows that it is quite difficult to change a long-held perception, even if that perception is wrong.

Judgments

Judgments are expressions of approval or disapproval. Like inferences, they are part of your report. As with inferences, those judgments supporting a previously held belief will be accepted quickly; whereas, judgments contrary to those beliefs will be resisted. If your judgments are of an adverse nature, they may be subject to distortion on the receiving end unless you take great pains to make them as clear and understandable as possible.

Pain and Pleasure

As humans, we respond to two basic forces—pain and pleasure. If you show a person that their actions are causing them to experience pain, they will do everything in their power to remove that pain. Likewise, if you show a person that their actions are causing pleasure, they will continue those actions. That's the way we are. As an auditor, you must show the pain resulting from nonconforming conditions.

Remembering that your customers are those managers in charge of the area being audited, you must show the pain in terms they can understand. This means you must find those adverse business conditions. Scrap, rework, missed deliveries, cut fingers, overtime, regulatory fines, and miscommunications are all examples of pain. Through the data-gathering phase, you have gathered a number of facts. The closer you can tie those facts to the goods and services being produced, the more successful you will be in convincing others that their actions are causing pain (or pleasure).

Findings

The majority of American audit programs use the term *finding* when presenting the unsatisfactory conclusions of an audit. Many audit program standards also use this word.[3] However, definition is lacking. Often, the term *finding* has a different meaning from one company or agency to another. In general, however, it means something bad. Seldom is a finding presented as a positive (or neutral) conclusion.

A finding is an audit conclusion that identifies a condition having a significant adverse effect on the quality of the activity under review. A finding has the following characteristics:

- It is negative. Something is amiss.

- It is a violation of a requirement. A promise was made at level 1, 2, 3 or 4, and it was not kept.

- It is significant. It is a big deal. It must somehow relate to business values and show how the problem is affecting those values in an adverse manner.

In the previous edition of this book, the term *audit observation* was presented as an adverse conclusion of a lesser nature. After noticing how this category of audit conclusion was being used around the country, it became obvious that something was wrong. Observations were being used to park the miscellaneous matters that were too difficult to deal with. They were one-time repositories of junk. Thinking was fading away. Also, the term was in conflict with the international standard on auditing, ISO 10011, published in 1991. For these reasons, *observation* as an audit conclusion has been removed. It is now used in this book in the same context as the international auditing standard. It is another term for an audit fact or a piece of data. It may be a good fact or a bad fact. Please refer to chapter 2 and the discussion of data for further details.

Other terms may be used for audit conclusions in your organization. Some of these other terms are *concern, major/minor noncompliance,* and *deficiency.* Because these words have not been defined in published audit program standards, you need to take steps to assure that the reader knows the meaning of the words being used. First, you should define each term in your local audit procedure. That way, you and other auditors in your group will be speaking the same language. Second, define the terms in your report. Do this by placing the definition in parentheses immediately after the first appearance of that word. That way, the reader will know exactly what you mean.

Preparing the Findings

Before your exit meeting (discussed later in this chapter), you need to assemble your team for one last, long, and serious caucus. Your goal is to develop the *finding statements* (if things are amiss) or *positive practice statements* (if things are swell) or both. Of course, if you don't have any findings or positive practices, you can go right into developing the overall summary. First, collect and discuss all of the good and bad facts uncovered during the course of the audit. Make a list of the bad facts. Don't attempt to figure out the causes and patterns yet; just write down all of the bad facts. Once your list is complete, write down the pain you have noticed. At this point you are starting to become subjective. That's OK, as long as the statements clearly show some pain within the area being audited. After you have identified the pain, write down the cause of that pain. Look at your list of adverse facts. Try to see the patterns and connections. Go back to the level 1 (policy) and level 2 (local description) standards to determine the larger areas of weakness. Remember the fishbone diagram and other statistical process control tools.[4]

Each finding must be a clear, concise statement of a generic problem, one that relates to a whole group, class, or activity. A single nonconformance, such as, "Printing software, being used for the generation of Starbird program reports, was not the current version," is not a finding. In this case the corrective action taken by the office will probably be limited to replacing that software module with the current version. No attempt will be made to find out why the obsolete version was being used in that group. Certainly, no effort will be taken to try to implement a software module control procedure, train personnel, or take other steps to address the underlying cause of this specific problem.

If there are a number of examples of incorrect versions in use, there is indeed a generic problem. But you still don't have a very strong case and haven't convinced management that a true problem exists. You need to show how similar problems fit into the picture. For example, a construction audit team might have gathered the following facts:

- Out of date blueprints were being used at seven of nine milepost work areas.

- The blueprint control register was last revised on March 6th, which is three months past the date required by Engineering Procedure 7.5.

- Red-lined drawings were noted in the guardrail fabrication shop, without evidence of approval authority. This is in violation of Engineering Procedure 3.6.

- 12 percent of the guardrails between mileposts 287 and 289 required rework.

- Field inspection change notices were not referenced on twelve blueprints in use, as required by Construction Order 6-2.

- Contractor rework of signal controls, costing $80,000, was due to the use of an incorrect specification.

All of these should be consolidated into one truly generic finding, such as: *"Work instruction documents are not effectively controlled. This is causing cost overruns and schedule delays."*

This finding statement should be followed by a brief restatement of the particular control element that is in need of attention—the quality program requirement for controlling documents in this example—and then a listing of the individual facts that show the basis for the statement. It is usually better to number each of the facts so that they may stand alone. Now, the discussion points show how the facts logically lead to the finding. A reasonable person (the reader) seeing those facts will draw the same conclusion that you have drawn.

A finding is a subjective opinion (judgment) supported by fact. Each of the facts, by themselves, may or may not be important. When they are combined, however, the reader can see the system failure. Findings are the disease; facts are the symptoms of that disease. This is the main difference between an audit and an inspection. Inspectors report problems. Auditors must analyze events for cause and effect. They show the management issues in need of correction. Inspection is part of the auditing process, but auditing is far more than inspection. Inspectors report nonconformances. Auditors tell us why those nonconformances happened.

This leads us to the last of the five basic *Rules* for quality audits:

5. Audit reports focus on the control system.

In order to serve our customers, we must show that the control systems either work or they do not work. Managers are looking for assurances that they are performing the tasks of planning, directing, and controlling in an effective fashion.

No Recommendations

Those who have had experience in auditing or have received audit reports, may have noted a significant departure from conventional practice, in that the term *recommendations* has yet to be used. When the audit group starts to provide solutions to another organization's management control problems, the inevitable result is a decrease in the quality of the product or service. There are several reasons for this.

Malicious Compliance

The receiving organization often does not know what you really mean in a *suggestion* and may be angry at you for making it in the first place. So they do an obviously stupid thing just to show you how far off base you are. Remember, the quickest way to get your boss in trouble is to do exactly what he or she says. Then you can always say, "I did just what you told me to do."

Inadequate Knowledge

Problems by their very nature are often difficult to solve. At times, this may require a very extensive analysis or an in-depth investigation. In the limited time for an audit, the team cannot always devote the resources necessary to find the true underlying cause(s) to a difficult problem, so the solution is inadequate. Don't be tempted to suggest some meaningless approaches for solving the problem, when you don't have enough information.

Perceived Bias

You may be tempted to suggest or recommend a solution based upon your prior experience in a similar situation. But because your solution was *not invented here*, it becomes suspect and you stand a chance of being accused of bias.

Ownership of Quality

If you allow yourself to recommend, suggest, or direct the necessary corrective action, then you have assumed at least partial ownership of the problem, with little or no resources to correct it. This is not an ideal position to be in. You have become a crutch for the management of the organization on the receiving end of the recommendation. Ownership of the quality of the product or service is no longer clearly defined; you have taken some of that ownership away. And when you take away ownership, you remove responsibility and accountability.

This concept of the ownership of quality is most important to success. Managers are paid good money to provide quality products and services and must be held accountable for the resulting work. The job of an auditor is to provide analyzed information—to be another set of eyes and ears for managers. You must find and analyze the true impediments to quality and then let affected managers and supervisors correct those problems. Does this mean that the auditors should just point out problems and then walk away? Of course not. But you must not impose your methods and approaches on the audited group. If asked, then you should certainly offer the benefit of your experience in having seen good and not-so-good methods.

If your firm requires that recommendations be placed in an audit report, then you should phrase them such that meaningful frameworks are provided without specific detail. In reality, recommendations are seldom optional. There is a great deal of pressure to do precisely what the auditor says, whether it contributes to quality or makes things worse. For most managers, there is a strong urge to keep a low profile. We seldom promote those who *rock the boat*. You should be aware of this reaction in your discussions with the auditee. Carefully phrase your conversations as solicited advice rather than required actions. Even though the report has yet to be issued, some of your utterances may become edict.

Remember that a finding is a condition adverse to quality. If not corrected, the quality of the group being evaluated will continue to suffer. Remember, too, that the main objective of an audit is to improve the performance of the area or activity being examined. This requires that findings be stated in terms that will arouse management interest and convince them that there are serious problems that must be investigated and corrected. Even though you have not made a direct recommendation for the fix, you have accomplished the same thing. The reader will see your words and want to change, because you have shown them (through the use of facts) the pain. However, they own that decision and its subsequent action.

Six or Less

Reports should generally be limited to six or fewer findings. We know that a small percentage of certain characteristics will account for a high percentage of certain problems. The importance of distinguishing the vital few from the trivial many can be seen in almost any situation.[5] For audits, this means that the vital few problems will make the major contribution to the lack of quality in most organizations.

Our poor little brains tend to overload when presented with too many problems simultaneously. As a result, none get the attention they truly deserve. Management can effectively address and resolve five problems; they cannot address 50.

If you discover that you continually report a large number of so-called findings, you are still inspecting. You have not determined the common management issue. You need to group several issues together. You need to analyze the situation further, to determine the system failures causing all of these discrepant items.

Overall Conclusions

Next, you need to develop an overall summary statement of everything you have examined. This is the bottom line. It includes the good as well as the bad. The credibility and acceptance of your message (and your written report) is substantially improved when it includes an evaluation of overall performance. "How well are we doing?" is a fair question, and some statement of analysis will go a long way in meeting the needs of your client. Remember, you're getting paid to answer the two basic questions of whether the control systems are in place and if they work. The summary is, therefore, the most important part of your entire report. Despite opinions to the contrary, it's OK to state that things are working well, like they should be, and that only a few minor problems exist.

Usually, a one-paragraph general discussion of the overall program controls is sufficient. Because your readers are managers, the words should be phrased in management terms. Here's an example for an audit of the training program.

> In general, the training program is being effectively implemented. Training needs have been defined. Adequate resources exist to provide identified training. Knowledge is demonstrated on the line and in the shops. However, in

the area of steam valve maintenance, some newly hired technicians were unsure of the proper stem lubricant to use.

Such a statement gives management a feeling of security in their implementation of this area. It also allows them to focus on the one remaining issue.

Exit Meeting

The exit meeting is the first formal opportunity for you to present your report to the group managers. Typically, the data-gathering part of the audit is concluded some time on the morning of the final day. The exit interview is then scheduled for some time in the afternoon, and you are left with about two to four hours to prepare something for the exit interview. If you have practiced the principle of no secrets, held daily caucuses, and kept the folks apprised of your progress and any concerns, this two-hour period is sufficient time to draft those findings, positive practices, and the summary.

Attendance

The exit meeting presentation should be made to the responsible managers of the group you just audited. On the other hand, attendance by several layers of management will most probably lead to argument. It is human nature to want to defend one's position in front of the boss, even if we know that position to be wrong. So a supervisor is obligated to argue a finding in his or her area if the director is present. Also, if they are at your meeting, they may well be away from more productive work. You can limit this arguing and unproductive time by requesting attendance by only senior group managers.

Conduct of the Meeting

The exit meeting is the job of the team leader. It's tough and demanding, but that's your job. Above all, avoid any arguing among the team members during the exit meeting. The team speaks with one voice—the team leader's.

As the team leader, you should start with a statement that the audit is finished. You then say the courtesy things, such as your appreciation for the hospitality extended to you and your team. State that you have accomplished your task. Then give your preview of coming attractions.

- Presentation of the summary
- Presentation of any findings and/or positive practices
- Corrections and explanations of any fuzzy areas
- Discussion of corrective action concepts and the follow-up process (if problems were identified)

Give a short recap of the audit scope and purpose and then get right into the summary. The best way to do this is in the form of a personal conversation between you, representing the team, and the senior auditee manager present. Look that person in the eye as you present the overall conclusions. Make that person feel that the subject matter is important and that the person is important as well. You should then present the highlights of any findings or positive practices. Don't go into great detail. Present the conclusion in a straightforward fashion, followed by the more significant facts. You should not have to present all of the individual items leading to your conclusion.

Draft Conclusions

At this point it is appropriate to pass out copies of the draft findings and/or positive practices. These are handwritten and assembled one to a page. There are several good reasons for doing this.

- It forces you to prepare for the exit meeting.
- It allows you to gather any remaining facts before you leave the audit area. Once the exit meeting is over, your access to additional data is severely limited.
- It keeps you honest. Often, you will be subjected to intense pressure to change your final report. For various reasons some will want you to go easy on them. Others will want you to get tough. By issuing your conclusions (in draft) at the exit meeting, you have committed yourself. You are in a better position to resist the pressure to change what was said at the exit meeting.

It is not necessary to make these draft conclusions perfect. Handwritten words on a lined tablet will do. Do not read the words out loud; rather, give them credit for being able to read by themselves. Explain the items in a conversational manner as briefly as you can, but remember that their listening abilities are diminished as they read the paper in front of them.

In preparing for the exit meeting, you should keep in mind that the facts and conclusions presented at the exit meeting must not be changed in the final report. If you have any concerns to raise, put them in your notes and discuss them in the exit meeting. Failure to do so, particularly if your facts are wrong, casts doubt on the entire audit effort.

Consider Their Viewpoint

In preparing for the exit meeting, it is worthwhile to put yourself in the readers' position and see things from their viewpoint. Remember that your objective is to change things for the better (or at least encourage the continuance of good practices). The art of the exit meeting lies in persuading the auditee (and your client) that your conclusions represent the true state of things. If problems were uncovered, then the consequences are serious and something can and should be done about them. It is a tough and demanding challenge for the team leader. Once finished, your whole team is physically, mentally, and emotionally exhausted. The team should promptly leave the area and disperse.

Process Audit Wrap-up Meeting

The preceding discussion deals with the larger, system audit. If you're doing a smaller, process audit, you don't need to assemble a large group of people. When you are finished with the fieldwork, go to a quiet place. Assemble your thoughts and compose your findings and/or positive practices. Think about the conclusion statement. Then go to the shift supervisor's office. Explain that your audit is finished, present your summary, and highlight any positive or negative conclusions. Then indicate that your report will be published within a week and leave promptly.

Formal Report

The formal report is the final communication of your audit to all three customers (auditee, client, organization). It must stand alone—a reasonably knowledgeable layman should be able to understand it without asking a series of questions. It should be issued within a reasonable time period after the exit meeting. Remember, the longer the report is held up in review, the more its importance diminishes to the auditee. You should issue the formal report for a system audit within two weeks of the exit meeting. One week should be sufficient for the process audit. These guidelines should not be difficult, if the practice of writing your conclusions (and perhaps summary) in draft before the exit meeting is observed.

Your written report should contain two to five sections.

- Introduction
- Overall summary
- Adverse conclusions (findings)
- Noteworthy accomplishments (positive practices)
- Attachments

The first two items, introduction and overall summary, are required in every report, even for the smaller, process audit. The last three items are optional, depending on the outcome.

Introduction

The report should begin with a short introduction. It tells the reader why the audit was performed (purpose), what was examined (scope), and who participated in the audit (auditors and auditees). Of course the purpose statement can be lifted directly from the previously issued audit plan. The scope should be brief, telling the reader what you looked at and the product of that activity. If this is a second-party, supplier audit, then give the plant location, relative size, and general customer base. When stating who did the auditing, list the audit team by name and identify the team leader. However, when discussing the auditee, it is best to avoid names. Otherwise, you are pointing fingers at specific individuals, should the results be less than outstanding. Rather, specify groups, activities, or locations. Doing so will lessen the adversarial nature of the audit process. The introduction paragraph should be about two inches long.

Overall Summary

The summary paragraph should come next. As stated earlier, this is the most important section of the report. It's the *bottom line* information to your customers. Are necessary controls present? Are they implemented across all activities? Do they work? Is the group achieving those higher level controls required for world-class quality? The summary section must answer these questions, but it must also be kept brief, clear, and concise if you are to retain your audience.

A summary will balance out the (by definition) negative tone of any findings. As humans, we respond much better to criticism when we are told that the overall program is working, but that there are a few areas in need of correction. The team will be recognized as competent and unbiased if the summary presents a professional, honest, and straightforward picture.

Adverse Conclusions

These are short, one- to two-sentence statements of each of the problem areas (findings), if there are any. When you have problems to report, this combination of summary and highlighted findings will get the attention of senior management. This includes managers from all three of your customers. If well prepared, it should stimulate interest in hearing about the details. It should lead to a desire to do something about any problems reported by the audit team.

Noteworthy Accomplishments

Sometimes, during the course of an audit, you will come across a group performing exceptionally well. Should this condition be reported? You bet it should! Don't, however, water down your report by calling everything exceptional. Remember that people and groups are expected to perform well. That's why we pay them a salary every month. However, you should acknowledge those program controls that are above and beyond the call of duty. Do this by devoting a separate paragraph to a description of the situation and how it affects the quality of the program under examination. Call this a positive practice and place it at the end of your report. This leaves the reader smiling.

Attachments

Next come the details for each finding and/or positive practice. Since you already passed these out in draft at the exit meeting, it's simply a matter of polishing up the words and making them look pretty. Present findings before positive practices and place the most important findings first. Your audience will devote the most attention to whatever you list first.

Arranging your findings by manual chapter or regulatory clause will inhibit your communication efforts.

Even though you may have many examples (facts) to support a particular finding, present only a page worth. You are no longer performing inspections. You are auditing. Your job is not to present the foreman with a list of discrepancies to *fix*. Your job is to convince through the judicious use of facts. Much like a debate, a few logically arranged facts will go far. When you get to the bottom of the page, stop writing and go on to the next finding.

Report Size

As an auditor, your job is to communicate to management. Your customers are busy people. Everyone else is throwing information at them. What makes you so special that they should stop everything and read your report for the next two hours? Nothing. If you want your report to be read, keep the size to two pages, plus any findings or positive practices as attachments (Figure 4.1). The process audit can be presented in one page plus attachments. Five pages will get read, but 50 pages will not reach your audience.

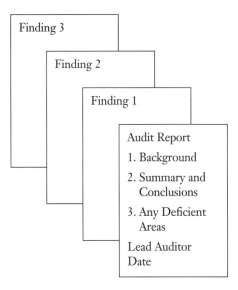

Figure 4.1. Audit report.

Report Distribution

You should not send the report directly to the auditee. Rather, attach it to a cover letter/memo issued by the client. This accomplishes three important objectives.

1. It forces the audit boss to read your report. Even if this individual wasn't there, he or she has a better understanding of the issues and can represent your audit group better in staff meetings.

2. It promotes accountability of the audit function. By signing the cover letter, the issuing manager owns a portion of the report, even if you drafted the cover letter. This ownership encourages the boss to look for clarity and other communication issues. Fairness is promoted. The overall excellence of the audit group is higher. Good reports are encouraged and poor reports are rewritten.

3. If you have any findings, the auditee will be asked to provide an action plan for fixing the problems. As a nonmanager, you have no authority to request such a response. For second-party, supplier audits, this is a contractual matter and must be done by the buyer or purchasing agent.

This is not to imply that your audit boss (client) must approve your team's audit report. This individual was not there and did not *smell the roses*; and, therefore, should not be asked to report on the aroma. The report is yours alone. However, your client (audit boss) is responsible for the adequacy and quality of your product. This can be accomplished through the normal supervisory review process without compromising your independence and integrity. Often, you may be requested to draft the cover memo (or letter) for the client's signature. The same concern with clear and effective communication applies here, as this is the first formal sheet of paper the auditee will see.

Recognizing that the process audit report may be as small as one sheet of paper, it doesn't make much sense to use the cover memo for these smaller reports. You prepare it, sign it, and then have the boss review it. This review is indicated by a signature and date under yours. You have accomplished the same objectives and saved a few trees.

Response Requested

If any problems were identified, the cover letter/memo should request a written response to all findings within a stated time. All requests for response should ask for four things.

1. Cause of the problem

2. Corrective action planned for the cause

3. Remedial action planned for each of the listed negative facts

4. Schedules and responsibilities for these actions

You are not asking that everything be fixed right away. Rather, you are asking for an action plan for correcting any problems. For second- and third-party audits, 30 days from receipt of the report is not an unreasonable time period for putting together this kind of information. For first-party, system audits, two to four weeks is reasonable. For first-party, process audits, one to two weeks is more appropriate. Regardless of the times, it is your responsibility, as the auditor, to specify *what is needed* and *when it is needed*. Don't make the reader refer to some procedure hidden away in another area for guidance on the response.

Distribution of the Report

Your report should go to only four places.

- Auditee

- Client

- Official files

- You and your team

Do not send your report out for wide distribution. If you send a copy to the auditee's manager, you are saying, "I don't trust you, so I'm going to tell your boss." If you send copies to their subordinates, you are saying, "I know better than you how to communicate to your group." Leave all of that further distribution to the auditee. Let the auditee decide if the results should be shared with one's boss and/or staff. It should be their call, not yours.

Wrap-up

In this section we considered the audit report as your *product*. It is the only permanent feature of all the work that goes into the audit. It is important that the report be written as the work progresses, not in a rush at the end.

The most important part of the audit report is the summary. This bottom line gives management of all parties an analysis of the health of the examined program from the audit team's perspective. Any problems identified through the audit must be presented so that management will take action on them. This requires that any findings address the truly important issues in business language. You must show the pain, if you want any change to occur. You must present information in a fashion that will lead the reader to draw the same conclusions as the audit team.

The exit meeting is the first formal presentation of the audit results, although everyone should have a pretty good idea of the results if the concept of no secrets (and daily briefings for system audits) has been implemented. Following the exit meeting, the formal report is issued.

Notes

1. Sawyer, Lawrence B. *The Practice of Modern Internal Auditing*, 2nd ed. (Altamonte Springs, Fla.: Institute of Internal Auditors, 1981): 434.

2. Cuzzetto, Charles E. "Auditing Management Reports," *Internal Auditor 45* (December 1988): 36.

3. The ISO 10011 auditing standard uses the British term *nonconformity* when referring to an adverse audit conclusion. The term *finding* does not appear in ISO 10011. The General Accounting Office publishes reports wherein significant deficiencies and problems are referred to as *findings*. The *Generally Accepted Government Auditing Standards* require copies of the audit report to go to those responsible for action on audit findings, implying something negative. The Institute of Internal Auditors, in their *Standards for the Professional Practice of Internal Auditing*, states that action should be taken on reported audit findings. They use the term *audit conclusions* in a generic fashion with neither positive nor negative connotation. The nuclear standard ANSI/ASME NQA-1 uses the term audit *finding* to denote an adverse condition requiring corrective action. Unfortunately, the author has been able to locate only one standard that specifically defines the term

finding. The *Generic Requirements for Auditing Nuclear Materials Safeguards Systems* (ANSI N15.38-1982), identifies a finding as a condition at variance with a requirement. In 1990 ASQC's Quality Auditing Technical Committee (now Quality Audit Division) developed a definition for *finding,* which subsequently appeared in its Certified Quality Auditor information booklet.

4. See chapter 2, note 2.

5. This phrase, *the vital few from the trivial many,* is often attributed to J. M. Juran. See J. M. Juran, ed., *Quality Control Handbook,* 3rd ed. (New York: McGraw-Hill, 1974): 2–16, for a discussion on its origin and use.

Chapter 5

Closure

Closure Phase

The closure phase of the audit starts after the formal report is issued. This phase covers

- Evaluation of the response
- Verification of the response
- Closing of the audit
- Assembly of the records

Because these items are intimately connected with the notion of corrective action, it is appropriate to begin by discussing the principles behind correcting problems.

Corrective Action

The principle of corrective action is that conditions adverse to quality must be identified and corrected. The cause must be determined. Steps must be taken to preclude repetition, including the reporting of these actions to management. True corrective action is difficult to implement, in that the real causes of problems are seldom easy to identify. But without an effective and objective corrective action program, the quality of all operations will suffer greatly.

Fundamental Components of Corrective Action

Any corrective action program has five fundamental components.

1. Identify the problem.
2. Identify the problem's cause.
3. Fix the problem.
4. Fix the cause of the problem.
5. Make sure the solutions work.

The audit program, along with inspection, will address the first step—finding problems. But as was discussed in the previous section on reporting, judgments must be made that may result in different interpretations on the severity of the reported problem. This is why the identification of *pain* is so important in the way findings are presented in your audit report. If you show the disease, rather than just the symptom, the cause becomes obvious. It is the underlying reason for the pain. It is the *cause* of cause-and-effect analysis.

When addressing the fixing of problems, immediate repair of the specific reported deficiency should not be confused with action taken to correct the cause of the problem and prevent its recurrence.[1] The function of a corrective action program is to analyze and remove these impediments to quality, safety, reliability, productivity, and so on. It must be a serious and continuous process.

Response to the Audit Report

After the audit report is issued, a response is requested from the auditee if any adverse conclusions (findings) are presented. This response is not a report that all problems have been fixed; rather, it sets forth the action to be taken. It is an action plan of things to come. For the second-party, system audit, 30 days from receipt of the audit report is the typical turn-around time for this response. For the first-party, system audit, 15 to 30 days is typical. For the small process audit, seven to 14 days is common. It is your duty, as the auditor, to make the response requirements and due dates very specific in the draft cover letter you prepare for the audit boss.

Although you may discuss corrective action issues in the exit meeting, you probably will not get much of a substantive commitment in that period of high stress. Senior managers want to think it over before they make any real promises to change. This is normal and to be expected.

It is usually the team leader's responsibility to keep track of the responses to an audit report if the audit has revealed one or more deficient items. If a response is not received by the requested date, you should first try a face-to-face meeting with the tardy manager(s). If this doesn't work, someone from your management/client team should call (or write if calls do not produce a response) to remind the audited organization of their need to positively commit to corrective action.

Adequacy of the Response

After receiving the response, your audit boss will turn the action plan over to you for evaluating its adequacy. This should be a team effort, if at all possible. You are looking for

- Identification of the underlying cause of the condition
- Plans for fixing the specific deficiencies, listed as facts under the finding statement
- Plans for fixing the underlying cause
- Identification of specific managers responsible for the above
- Due dates for accomplishing the corrections

Personal preference should not influence this evaluation; you must decide if the planned action makes sense and has a reasonable chance of success. At this point you should probably ease up on your expectations. You have expended most of your energy and persuasion devices. If things look like they will get better, accept the response.

In a very real way the response you receive from the auditee is your direct measure of performance as an auditor. If you write a good report, one that relates to business values and communicates to senior management, you will receive a good response. If your response is argumentative, you should look at yourself, rather than the auditee. (When you point your finger at someone, three of your fingers are pointing back to you.) What did you do to cause that miscommunication? How can you do better next time? The response is your report card.

Communication Back to the Auditee

Of course, you should keep the auditee informed of the status of their audit and your intentions. Do this by drafting a memo from the audit boss to the auditee. State that the response was found to be acceptable and that further examination will be scheduled to verify completion of promised actions. The concept of no secrets doesn't end after the exit meeting. If the auditee has taken the time and effort to provide a response, they deserve some sort of acknowledgment; otherwise, reaction to the next audit may be less than enthusiastic.

There are, however, times when the response is judged inadequate. Once this has been decided, and your informal discussions are getting nowhere, you must ask for help from the client (audit boss or contract administrator). It is here that the true strength of your audit program will show. If your client truly believes in the value of auditing, they will back you up (and council you to produce better reports in the future). Working with your client and other affected managers, you should draft a letter/memo stating why the response is deemed to be unacceptable and requesting a new response. The tone of this letter should be significantly more forceful than before.

If serious doubts about the effectiveness of corrective action plans continue and your management is unable to sway the auditee by discussion, request your client to schedule a follow-up visit with the auditee to work out the problems. As a last resort for suppliers, your firm may wish to make effective corrective action on the findings a precondition for the auditee to be considered for any additional business. Such drastic action should be viewed as an indication that the audit has failed in its original purpose.

Closeout

Once the response has been analyzed and found to be acceptable, promised corrective action must be verified in some fashion. Several options are available to you.

1. The response adequately describes the conditions of change and there is a reasonable chance of success. Accept the response and close out that finding immediately.

2. Some promised changes involve new or revised documents. Request that these changed documents be forwarded to you once issued. Providing the changed documents meet the requirements, the finding may be closed.

3. It may be necessary for someone from your organization to perform a brief follow-up visit to personally verify the implementation of the

promised corrective action. This person may be a member of the audit team, an affected person from another group (such as the project engineer), or a third party.

This follow-up must be limited to just inspection of the promised corrective action. You are no longer in an audit mode. You should not examine the situation for effectiveness at this point. Assuming things are satisfactory, a record is made of the satisfactory inspection and the finding is closed.

Periodic Status Reports

A very useful technique in tracking action on audit results is to issue periodic audit status reports. These should identify

- The status of each finding (open or closed) for each audit (internal and external)
- Target dates for responses and corrective actions
- The overall status of the audit (open or closed)

Such reports can help your management assess the status of actions on audit results; and (at least for internal audits) may stimulate the audited groups to get moving.

Formal Closure

When all findings have been closed, the audit should be formally closed by letter or memo. This is basic courtesy as well as good business practice. The auditee is probably tracking the audit and wondering if all is in order. As before, the letter or memo will be prepared by you and signed by the client. In case of corrective actions that may be deferred for long periods, or where their completion cannot be determined without a follow-up audit, the individual audit should be closed and follow-up provided by other means, such as the audit status report or commitment control system. Finally, all corrective action should be examined at the next regularly scheduled audit of that area.

Records

With good records, it should be relatively easy to convince others of the effectiveness of your audit program. You examine records in your quest for the truth; others will do likewise. In addition, good records will help when preparing for the next regularly scheduled audit.

Audit records may be classified as either long-term or short-term records, depending upon their use and the length of time they are kept. While practices vary throughout the nation, a good length of time to keep long-term records is five years. After that, the records probably won't mean very much to you and most outside examiners. If you are in a regulated industry, such as pharmaceuticals or nuclear power, check with your legal staff or contract administrators.

The following items are candidates for long-term records:

- Audit notification letter and audit plan
- Blank checklists
- Audit report and cover letter
- Response from the auditee
- Finding follow-up inspection results
- Closing letter

Short-term records are kept mainly for your own use. They are not really used to prove anything. A good length of time to keep these records is one year or until the next audit of that area. Candidates for short-term records include the following:

- Copies of auditor qualification records
- Completed checklists (work papers)
- Documents and records obtained from auditee
- Additional correspondence

You may have noticed that completed checklists are not in the long-term category. Often, untrained auditors will examine your files, pull out your five-year-old notes, and ask why certain decisions were made. By periodically purging these limited-use records, you have fewer sources of unnecessary discomfort.

A good way to keep your records is to assemble everything from a particular audit into two folders—long-term and short-term. Set aside one file cabinet or file drawer for these audit records. Then before completely closing an audit, assemble all the necessary records and place them in the proper folder. Periodically, folders may be purged to make room for new ones.

A Recap

In this chapter we considered the activities following the reporting phase. These activities include evaluating the auditee's response, verifying completion of the promised corrective action, keeping the auditee informed of the status of the audit, and assembling the necessary records.

The evaluation of the auditee's response is perhaps the most difficult part of the closeout action. If there is a reasonable chance of success (improved performance), then the response should be accepted.

Notes

1. Vice Admiral Rickover of the U.S. Navy nuclear submarine fleet used to say that "problems have half-lives," meaning that they will always recur due to an everchanging environment. For this reason it is often stated that corrective actions should minimize the chance of recurrence, rather than prevent recurrence.

Chapter 6

Postscript

You have seen how the basic monitoring methods originally developed by accountants can be used to improve any type of activity, large or small, internal or external. The keys to success are no different here than in any other business venture.

- Thorough preparation
- Rigorous performance
- Meaningful reporting
- Effective follow-up

Whether you perform audits of the processes used to make various items, the performance of other departments, or the actions of your suppliers, you use the same basic auditing skills. These skills are developed by formal training coupled with real-life practice. Skilled auditors are one of your company's or agency's greatest assets. They know the processes, people, and procedures. They understand internal and external customer relationships. And they possess the ability to communicate to management.

Ideally, auditors should possess a balance of emotional, mechanical, and intellectual skills. They must be able to conduct interviews, control a hostile group, convince a skeptical audience, and understand different perspectives. They must also be skilled in the mechanics of sampling, tracing, analysis, and other forms of data processing. Finally, they must be able to organize a campaign and communicate to their fellow humans. These are not easy skills to obtain. They can only be developed through study, practice, and feedback.

It is the responsibility of the manager in charge of the audit program to demand excellence and provide feedback. If one allows poor reports to be published, then eventually all reports will achieve that level of mediocrity. If the audit program does not contribute to the betterment of the firm or agency, it should not be allowed to survive. Thus, it is important to always remember that the goal of auditing is to improve the performance of the audited activity.

Auditing can be distilled down to five fundamental rules.

1. Auditing is a function of management.

2. Auditors are qualified to perform their tasks.

3. Measurements are taken against defined standards.

4. Conclusions are based on fact.

5. Audit reports focus on the control system.

Periodically, you should examine your own audit program to see if these rules are still being followed.

This text has presented some basic concepts and theories of the quality audit process. It has also attempted to present some practical ways of implementing the theory. As the application of quality auditing becomes more established, certain methods will grow and others will die. This is to be expected. Auditing, like all the soft sciences, is an evolutionary process. Regardless of the changes, though, the purpose of the audit will always be to provide management with meaningful information upon which to base decisions. Through proper application, these decisions will cause performance to improve.

Example Internal System Audit Procedure

Purpose and Scope

This procedure is intended to cover the planning and execution of internal system audits. Internal process audits are under the control of each functional department and are controlled through the use of functional department procedures. This procedure does not address auditing of external suppliers, or the manner in which we respond to audits performed on our activities by others.

Definitions

Lead Auditor—A person who is qualified and authorized to manage and direct an audit. Also known as an Audit Team Leader.

Auditor—A person who is qualified to assist a Lead Auditor in performing a portion of an audit assignment. Also known as an Audit Team Member.

Audit Finding—An audit conclusion that identifies a condition having a significant adverse effect on the quality of the activity under review.

Audit Observation—A statement of fact, either good or bad.

Document—A written description of an activity to be accomplished.

Record—A written description of an activity that has been accomplished.

Personnel Qualification

Lead Auditors shall be qualified to the provisions of ANSI/ASQC Q10011, Part 2, Qualification Criteria for Quality Systems Auditors. Auditors shall be qualified to the requirements specified by the audit's TEAM LEADER.

Scheduling

Internal system audits shall be performed in a cost-effective manner consistent with the needs of internal and external customers and available resources. Annual audit planning shall be conducted in the first quarter after the new fiscal year. By the end of the first quarter of each year, the AUDITS MANAGER shall prepare an Annual Audit Planning Schedule based upon the following criteria:

1. Cost—High-dollar activities shall be audited before low-dollar areas. Factors to consider should be contract amount, personnel assigned, importance to some national effort, and potential for scrap or waste.

2. Risk—High-risk activities shall receive priority in audit planning. Factors to consider should be safety to employees, potential for environmental damage, and possible loss of capital equipment.

3. Management Requests—Those areas receiving the greatest management attention should be audited before areas in need of little attention. The needs of the customer shall also be considered.

4. Department or Section—At least one audit shall be scheduled each year to examine the implementation of the company QA program within each Department or Section. This is considered to be above and beyond the annual appraisal of QA program effectiveness required by company policy.

5. Administrative Activity—Because the following activities affect all projects and programs within the company, they shall be scheduled individually. Other activities may be added as required.

   • Procurements

   • Records management

   • Document control

   • General employee training

The Annual Audit Planning Schedule shall identify audited activities and the month in which they are scheduled for audit. No further definition (specific dates, auditors, requirements, and so on) is required or desired. The Annual Audit Planning Schedule shall be approved by the PLANT MANAGER and distributed to all departments and sections within the company, and to affected customers when required, by the QUALITY ASSURANCE DIRECTOR. The Annual Audit Planning Schedule may be modified but once before a new schedule must be prepared and distributed.

Quarterly Audit Planning Schedules shall be developed by the AUDITS MANAGER, based upon the annual audit planning schedule. These quarterly schedules shall contain the following information:

- Audited activity (from annual schedule)
- Start date
- Audit team leader

Quarterly schedules shall be distributed by the AUDITS MANAGER, to all affected project or program managers, and others as deemed necessary, prior to the start of each quarter. These schedules may be modified to suit circumstances, as long as all planned audits are performed within the affected quarter. Should any audits appearing on the annual plan be deferred during the affected quarter, the reason for such deferral shall be reported to the QUALITY ASSURANCE DIRECTOR.

Audit Planning

Prior to the performance of an audit, an Audit Plan shall be prepared and appropriate parties shall be notified. Audit Plans shall be prepared by the audit team leader and contain the following information:

- Audit title and number
- Auditee
- Purpose
- Scope
- Performance standards
- Organizations affected
- Any interfaces

- Team members
- Overall schedule
- Review and approval

The audit plan shall be reviewed by another auditor. The audit team leader shall sign and date the audit plan to indicate approval. Additionally, the lead auditor shall draft a notification memo from the AUDITS MAN-AGER to the affected activity manager(s). The notification memo should summarize the information contained in the Audit Plan and include the Plan as an attachment. Every effort should be made to notify the auditee, in writing, at least 30 days in advance of an impending audit. Audit team members should also receive a copy of the notification memo and Plan.

Written checklist questions shall be developed for each audit prior to the commencement of the audit (opening meeting). These checklist questions shall act as a guide to the audit team in performing their investigation in order to assure that all important elements of the control system are examined. As such, they may be written in any format found to be useful to the individual auditor(s). They shall, however, include examination questions covering each control element specified in the audit base (requirements documents). Checklists shall be developed individually for each audit, but may include questions from previous audits and standard lists. In order to provide for added assurance that checklist questions are adequate for the audited area, each checklist shall be reviewed by a qualified lead auditor, other than the preparer. This review shall be indicated by the words *reviewed* and a signature and date somewhere on the front page of each checklist. Checklists may be informally provided to the auditee prior to the fieldwork.

Performance

Fieldwork shall commence with a brief opening meeting between the audit team and the management of the area to be audited. Blank copies of the checklists to be used for the audit shall be distributed at the opening meeting. (This is in addition to any informal copies provided earlier.) The audit shall be performed such that elements selected for examination are evaluated for conformance and effectiveness against specified requirements. Objective evidence shall be examined to the degree necessary to determine if the control elements are being effectively implemented. The results of this examination (positive and negative facts) should be recorded on the checklist pages or on supplemental notes. Every effort should be made to keep the auditee apprised of the progress of the audit and concerns of the audit team. For audits lasting longer than a day, the auditee shall be briefed at the end of each day.

Audit Report

Each audit shall conclude with a brief closing (exit) meeting between the audit team and the management of the area audited. Copies of the draft audit conclusions (or summary), along with any draft Findings or Positive Practices should be provided to those in attendance.

Within one week of the audit closing meeting, the Audit Report shall be prepared in the form of a memo from the AUDIT TEAM LEADER to the AUDITS MANAGER. The Audit Report shall contain the following information:

- Audit title, number, and other identifying information
- Background information, such as audit purpose, scope, dates, audit team members, and procedures used, plus a brief description of the activities audited and any affected customers (one paragraph)
- Summary and overall conclusions of the effectiveness of the quality program as implemented by the audited organization(s)
- An executive summary of any Findings or Positive Practices and how they affect products or deliverables
- Specific Findings or Positive Practices as attachments

Audit Findings shall be presented as a generic statement of the non-conforming condition and its affect on business operations. This is followed by discussion (or explanation) points, the first of which should be a description of the specific requirement(s) for the control item under question. Then list two or more examples of specific objective evidence, found during the course of the audit, supporting the conclusion that a significant adverse condition exists.

Positive Practices shall be presented in a fashion similar to Audit Findings, except that examples cited are good, rather than bad, practices.

The Audit Report shall be provided to the affected manager(s) by a cover memo from the AUDITS MANAGER. The cover memo shall request corrective action as applicable. If the report includes any Audit

Findings, a blank Audit Finding Response Form shall be included for use by the addressee. Generally, a response to an audit report should be requested such that a reply is received within 30 days of the audit report date. Additional copies of the cover memo and report should be provided to the audit team members and the audit files.

Follow-up

Responses shall be evaluated by the AUDIT TEAM LEADER for effective corrective action that addresses the concerns expressed by the audit report. Specifically, replies to Audit Findings shall be evaluated to verify that

- The cause of the problem has been identified.
- Actions have been (or will be) taken to correct the specific problem areas (Remedial Action).
- Actions have been (or will be) taken to correct the cause of the problem (Corrective Action).
- Specific responsibilities and dates for corrective action have been identified.

Once the above has been obtained and any follow-up verification has been completed, the AUDIT TEAM LEADER shall complete the bottom of the Audit Finding Response Form to indicate that the Audit Finding has been closed.

The AUDITS MANAGER shall be periodically apprised of the status of outstanding Audit Findings. Appropriate steps, including involvement of the Director of Quality Assurance, shall be taken to resolve outstanding audit issues. After all of an audit's Findings have been closed, the AUDIT TEAM LEADER shall prepare a closing notice for the AUDITS MANAGER to sign and send to the affected auditee manager(s).

Records

The following items are considered to be long-term audit records and shall be maintained by the AUDITS MANAGER for five years:

- Audit Notification Memo and Audit Plan
- Blank Audit Checklists

- Audit Report and Forwarding Memo
- Audit Response, including completed Audit Finding Response Forms
- Closure Memo

The following items are considered to be working audit records and shall be maintained by the AUDITS MANAGER for a period of one year, after which time they may be discarded:

- Inactive Auditor/Lead Auditor Qualification Records
- Completed Audit Checklists and auditor's working papers
- Related miscellaneous correspondence
- Annual Audit Schedules and any revisions
- Quarterly Audit Schedules
- Superseded Auditing Procedures (marked *archive*)

Forms

Examples of forms used in the administration of the audit program are attached. These may be modified at the discretion of the AUDITS MANAGER.

Appendix B

Glossary of Terms

Appraisal—A form of the quality system audit, normally conducted to examine the total quality program effectiveness and implementation. An appraisal is often conducted by a third party and reported to the very highest levels of management.

Assessment—A European term for the quality system audit.

Audit—An independent, structured, and reported check to see that something is as it should be. An audit may examine any portion of the management control spectrum, including financial, environmental, and quality aspects of business and government.

Audit program—The methods used to plan and perform audits.

Audit standard—A written description of essential audit characteristics, reflecting current thought and practice.

Audit team—A group of individuals conducting an audit under the direction of a team leader.

Auditee—The organization to be audited. The auditee may be another group within the firm/agency or it may be an entirely separate organization.

Auditor—A person who is qualified to assist a Lead Auditor in performing a portion of an audit assignment. Also known as an Audit Team Member.

Certification (of auditors and lead auditors)—The act of determining, verifying, and attesting to the qualifications of a person to perform effective audits in accordance with applicable requirements. Certification may be internal (by the person's employer) or external (by a professional society such as the American Society for Quality Control or the Institute of Internal Auditors).

Characteristic—Any distinct property of an item or activity that can be described and measured.

Client—The person or organization requesting or sponsoring an audit. Typically, the client is the person in charge of the internal and/or supplier audit program.

Confirmation—The agreement of data obtained from two or more different sources.

Corrective action—Action taken to eliminate the causes of an existing undesirable condition, in order to minimize or prevent its recurrence.

Corroboration—Confirmation of information obtained by an interview.

Desk audit—The evaluation of lower-tier documents to higher-tier standards before fieldwork starts.

Document—A written description of an activity to be accomplished. (*See also* Record.)

Evaluation—The act of examining a process or group to some standard and forming certain conclusions as a result.

Examination—A measurement of goods, services, or knowledge to determine conformance to some standard.

External audit—A second-party audit performed on your supplier by you.

Extrinsic audit—A second-party audit performed on you by your customer.

Finding—An audit conclusion that identifies a condition having a significant adverse effect on the quality of the activity under review. An audit finding contains both cause and effect and is normally accompanied by several specific examples of the observed condition.

Follow-up—Verifying that some corrective action has been accomplished as promised.

Guidelines—Methods that are considered good practice but that are not mandatory. Generally, the term *should* denotes a guideline and the term *shall* denotes a mandatory requirement.

Independent—Not directly responsible for the quality, cost, and/or production of goods and services being examined.

Inspection—Activities (such as measuring, examining or testing) gauging one or more characteristics of a product or service, and comparing these with specified requirements to determine conformity.[1]

Lead auditor—A person who is qualified and authorized to manage and direct an audit. Also known as an audit team leader.

Nonconformity—The nonfulfillment of specified requirements.[2] This term is popular in Europe as a substitute for *finding*. It addresses compliance, but does not often address effectiveness. A *major nonconformity* is cause to fail a third-party registration audit. A *minor nonconformity* is a deficiency in need of correction before the registration certificate will be issued.

Objective evidence—Qualitative or quantitative information, records or statements of fact, pertaining to the quality of an item or service or to the existence and implementation of a quality system element, which is based on observation, measurement or test, and which can be verified.[3]

Observation—A statement of fact made during an audit and substantiated by objective evidence.[4] An observation may be a good fact or a bad fact.

Process audit—The evaluation of a process operation against established instructions and product standards. The process audit measures conformance to product standards and effectiveness of process instructions. It is sometimes called a *surveillance*.

Product audit—A reinspection and retest of product that has already been accepted or a review of records for that product. It is not a true *audit*, but rather an *inspection*. It is sometimes called a *[shipping] dock audit*.

Quality assurance—All those planned and systematic actions necessary to provide adequate confidence that a product or service will satisfy given requirements for quality.[5]

Quality audit—A systematic and independent examination to determine whether quality activities (and related results) comply with planned arrangements and whether these arrangements are implemented effectively and suitable for achieving objectives.[6] (Author's Note: This definition contains the three concepts of compliance, effectiveness, and suitability.)

Record—A written description of an activity that has been accomplished. (*See also* Document.)

Specification—A set of requirements to be satisfied by a specific product or service. A specification is a level 4 document.

Standard—A government- or industry-endorsed description of essential characteristics of an item or activity. Standards may be product specific (such as ASCII for computer data exchange), user specific (such as ISO 10011 for quality system audits), or generic (such as ANSI/ASQC Q9002 for general supplier-customer relationships).

Surveillance—(*See* Process Audit.)

Survey—An activity conducted prior to a contract award and used to evaluate the overall quality capability of a prospective supplier or contractor.

System audit—A structured activity performed to verify that one or more portions of a quality program are appropriate and are effectively implemented in accordance with agreed-to standards of performance. (Use of the term *quality systems audit* is incorrect. Only one quality system can be audited at a time.)

Notes

1. *ISO 8042: Quality—Vocabulary.* (Geneva: International Organization for Standardization, 1986).

2. See note 1.

3. *ISO 10011-1: Guidelines for Auditing Quality Systems.* (Geneva: International Organization for Standardization, 1990).

4. See note 3.

5. See note 1.

6. See note 1.

ISO 9001 Conspectus

1. Management Responsibility
   a. Quality Policy shall be defined, documented, understood, implemented, and maintained.
   b. Responsibilities and authorities for all personnel specifying, achieving, and monitoring quality shall be defined. In-house verification resources shall be defined, trained, and funded. Designated management person to see that quality program is implemented and maintained.
   c. Quality program shall be periodically reviewed to assure its suitability and effectiveness.

2. Quality System
   a. Procedures shall be prepared.
   b. Procedures shall be implemented.

3. Contract Review
   a. Incoming contracts (& POs) shall be reviewed to see if requirements are adequately defined, they agree with the bid, and they can be implemented.

4. Design Control
  a. The design project shall be planned.
  b. Design input parameters shall be defined.
  c. Design output, including crucial product characteristics, shall be documented.
  d. Design output shall be verified to meet input requirements.
  e. Design changes shall be controlled.

5. Document Control
  a. Generation of documents shall be controlled.
  b. Distribution of documents shall be controlled.
  c. Changes to documents shall be controlled.

6. Purchasing
  a. Potential subcontractors and subsuppliers shall be evaluated for their ability to provide stated requirements.
  b. Requirements shall be clearly defined in contracting data.
  c. Effectiveness of the subcontractor's QA system shall be assessed.

7. Customer-supplied Material
  a. Any customer-supplied material shall be protected against loss or damage.

8. Product Identification and Traceability
  a. The product shall be identified and traceable by item, batch or lot, during all stages of production, delivery, and installation.

9. Process Control
  a. Production (and installation) processes shall be defined and planned.
  b. Production shall be carried out under controlled conditions: documented instructions, in-process controls, approval of processes and equipment, and criteria for workmanship.
  c. Special processes, which cannot be verified after-the-fact, shall be monitored and controlled throughout the processes.

10. Inspection and Testing
  a. Incoming material shall be inspected or verified before use.
  b. In-process inspection and testing shall be performed.
  c. Final inspection and testing shall be performed prior to release of finished product.
  d. Records of inspection and test shall be kept.

11. Inspection, Measuring, and Test Equipment

a. Equipment used to demonstrate conformance shall be controlled, calibrated, and maintained.
- identify measurements to be made
- identify affected instruments
- calibrate instruments (procedures, status indicators)
- periodically check calibration
- assess measurement validity if found out of calibration
- control environmental conditions in metrology lab

b. Measurement uncertainty and equipment capability shall be known.

c. Where test hardware or software is used, they shall be checked before use and rechecked during use.

12. Inspection and Test Status

a. Status of inspections and tests shall be maintained for items as they progress through various processing steps.

b. Records shall show who released conforming product.

13. Control of Nonconforming Product

a. Nonconforming products shall be controlled to prevent inadvertent use or installation.

b. Review and disposition of nonconforming product shall be accomplished in a formal manner.

14. Corrective Action

a. Problem causes shall be identified.

b. Specific problems and their causes shall be corrected.

c. Effectiveness of corrective actions shall be assessed.

15. Handling, Storage, Packaging, and Delivery

a. Procedures for handling, storage, packaging, and delivery shall be developed and maintained.

b. Handling controls shall prevent damage and deterioration.

c. Secure storage shall be provided. Product in stock shall be checked for deterioration.

d. Packing, preservation, and marking processes shall be controlled.

e. Quality of the product after final inspection shall be maintained. This may include delivery controls.

16. Records

a. Quality records shall be identified, collected, indexed, filed, stored, maintained, and dispositioned.

17. Internal Quality Audits
    a. Audits shall be planned and performed.
    b. Results of audits shall be communicated to management.
    c. Any deficiencies found shall be corrected.

18. Training
    a. Training needs shall be identified.
    b. Training shall be provided.
    c. Selected tasks may require qualified individuals.
    d. Records of training shall be maintained.

19. Servicing
    a. Servicing activities shall be performed to written procedures.
    b. Servicing activities shall meet requirements.

20. Statistical Techniques
    a. Statistical techniques shall be identified.
    b. Statistical techniques shall be used to verify acceptability of process capability and product characteristics.

ISO 9001-1987 Audit Checklist

Note of Caution

This checklist only covers the essential elements of ISO 9001-1987. Because it only covers the highest (policy) level of possible performance standards, it must never be used without modification. Local application requirements from level 2–4 standards must be added to the questions prior to use on an actual audit.

(All references are to Section 4, Quality System Requirements)

1   Management Responsibility

1.1   Quality Policy

1 Does a written policy on quality exist?
2 Have management objectives for quality been defined?
3 Is there any method of showing management commitment to quality?
4 Has the quality policy been transmitted and explained to all levels of the organization?

1.2   Organization

1.2.1   Responsibility and Authority

1 Have personnel who manage, perform, and/or verify work affecting quality been identified?

2 Are responsibilities defined and authority established for personnel who manage, perform, and/or verify work affecting quality?

3 Is there a person or group with the authority to initiate action to prevent the occurrence of product nonconformity?

4 Is there a person or group with the authority to identify and/or record product quality problems?

5 Is there a person or group with the authority to initiate, recommend, and provide solutions through designated channels?

6 Is there a means to verify the effectiveness of these solutions?

7 Is there a person or group with the authority to control further processing, delivery, or installation until deficiencies or unsatisfactory conditions are corrected?

1.2.2 Verification Resources and Personnel

1 Have in-house verification requirements and activities been identified?

2 Are resources for these verification activities provided?

3 Are trained personnel assigned to these verification activities?

4 Are design reviews and audits performed by personnel independent of those having direct responsibility for the work performed?

1.2.3 Management Representative

1 Is there one individual responsible for ensuring that ISO 9001 requirements are implemented and maintained?

1.3 Management Review

1 Does management review the quality system to ensure its continuing suitability and effectiveness?

2 Are intervals between reviews specified and observed?

3 Are records of these reviews maintained?

4 Do these reviews include assessment of the results of internal quality audits?

2 Quality System

1 Do written quality system procedures and instructions exist?

2 Do these procedures and instructions cover all elements of ISO 9001?

3 Are quality system procedures and instructions being maintained?

4 Has a quality manual been prepared? Is it being used?

*Customize prior to use

5 Are quality plans prepared? Are they used?

6 Have controls and processes needed to achieve required quality been identified? Are they in place?

7 Has the inspection equipment (and fixturing) been identified? Has it been acquired?

8 Are the identified skills needed to achieve required quality in place?

9 Is there a means for updating quality control, inspection, and testing techniques?

10 Is new instrumentation developed to meet changing needs?

11 Is there a means to identify needed improvements (beyond state-of-art) in measurement requirements capability?

12 Are standards of acceptability clear? This includes subjective standards.

13 Is there a means to assess the compatibility of design, production process, installation, inspection and test procedures, and applicable documentation?

3   Contract Review

1 Are there written procedures for contract review? Are they being used?

2 Are contracts reviewed to ensure that customer requirements are defined and documented?

3 Are contracts reviewed to ensure that customer requirements different from those in the tender (bid) are resolved?

4 Are contracts reviewed to ensure that the capability to meet customer requirements exists?

5 Are records of contract reviews maintained?

6 Are interface mechanisms between the purchaser (customer) and supplier (company) clear for this contract review process?

7 Select [a number of] contracts/purchase orders received within the past [year] and verify that internal work/production orders agree with customer requirements.

4   Design Control

4.1   General

1 Are there written procedures for control and verification of the product design? Are they being used?

*Customize prior to use

4.2   Design and Development Planning

    1 Do project plans exist that identify the responsibility for each design and/or development activity (function/group/individual)?

    2 Are these project plans updated as the design evolves?

4.2.1   Activity Assignment

    1 Is there a documented plan for design and design verification activities?

    2 Are there qualification criteria for design and verification personnel?

    3 Are design and verification activities assigned to staff who meet these criteria?

    4 Are design and verification staff equipped with resources sufficient to perform their jobs?

4.2.2   Organizational and Technical Interfaces

    1 Are the organizational and technical planning interfaces between different design/verification groups identified? (This may include customer interface.)

    2 Is project information documented, transmitted, and regularly reviewed?

4.3   Design Input

    1 Are product/project requirements documented?

    2 Have the requirements been reviewed for adequacy?

    3 Are the requirements clear and consistent?

    4 Select a recent design project and verify that input requirements are documented and clear.

4.4   Design Output

    1 Is design output documented in terms of requirements, calculations, and/or analyses?

    2 Is design output assessed for conformance with design input requirements?

    3 Does design output contain or reference acceptance criteria? (This may include items such as performance target values, tolerances and attributes, durability, safety, reliability, maintainability under storage and operating conditions, validation of computer systems and software, statistical validation of tests/inspections to the appropriate confidence level, and so on.)

*Customize prior to use

4 Is design output formally assessed for conformance to regulatory requirements? (These may include safety, fire, environmental, health, building codes, and so on.)

5 Does the design output identify those requirements which are crucial to the safe and proper functioning of the product? (These may include reliability and maintainability, serviceability for the product (project) life cycle, project/product failure, decomposition, safe disposal, and so on.)

6 Select a recent design project and verify that output results meet input requirements.

4.5   Design Verification

1 Are there documented criteria for design verification?

2 Have the functions for verifying the design been planned, established, documented, and assigned to specific personnel?

3 Does design verification establish that design output meets design input requirements? (This may include design reviews, qualification tests, alternative calculations, or comparison to similar designs.)

4.6   Design Changes

1 Are there written procedures to identify and document all changes and/or modifications in the design? Are they being used?

2 Do procedures require review and formal approval of all design changes and/or modifications?

3 Are design change procedures being used?

5   Document Control

5.1   Document Approval and Issue

1 Are there written procedures to control all documents and data related to ISO 9001 requirements? (that is, Are there procedures for procedures?) Are they being used?

2 Have documents/data falling under these control requirements been identified?

3 Are these controlled documents reviewed and approved prior to use?

4 Do authorized personnel perform these reviews and approvals? Have authorized personnel been identified?

*Customize prior to use

5 Are documents (procedures, instructions, data) available to personnel operating the process? (that is, Those performing the work need instructions.)

6 Are obsolete documents promptly removed from all points of issue or use?

7 Select [number] procedures, specifications, or drawings and verify that they have been approved and are available.

5.2 Document Changes/Modifications

1 Are document changes reviewed and approved by the same functions/organizations that performed the original review?

2 Do these functions/organizations have access to pertinent background information upon which to base their review and approval?

3 Is the nature of the changes identified in the documents? (This may not be practicable.)

4 Is there a master list which identifies the current revision of documents?

5 Is this master list accessible to users so that they do not use non-applicable documents?

6 Are documents reissued to incorporate accumulated changes?

7 Select [number] procedures, specifications, or drawings and verify that the correct version is being used.

6 Purchasing

6.1 General

1 Is there a system in place to ensure that incoming purchased material conforms to specified requirements? (Examples of ways to accomplish this include: receiving inspection, test verification, performance evaluation and test, process capability results, supplier verification (Certificate of Compliance or Conformance), preshipment (source) inspection, and supplier audit. See also Receiving Inspection below.)

6.2 Assessment of Subcontractors

1 Are subcontractors selected on the basis of their ability to meet subcontract requirements, including quality requirements?

2 Are there records (or a list) of acceptable subcontractors?

*Customize prior to use

3 Does the type and extent of control over subcontractors vary according to the type of product, or record of demonstrated capability?

4 Is there a means of ensuring that subcontractor quality system controls are effective? (This may be by audit, periodic review of history, or other means.)

5 Choose [number] subcontractors and verify that they were approved when orders were placed.

6.3   Purchasing Data

1 Do purchasing documents (contracts and purchase orders) uniquely describe the product ordered? (This may be type, class, style, grade, model, part number, and so on.)

2 Are reference documents identified by title and issue? These include specifications, drawings, process requirements, and inspection instructions.

3 Are requirements for approval or qualification of product, procedures, processing equipment and personnel clearly described?

4 Is the quality system standard identified in purchase documents? (This may be one of the ISO 9000 series or other recognized standards.)

5 Are purchasing documents reviewed and approved against documented criteria prior to release?

6 Select [number] purchase orders within the last [year] and verify that the above five items have been accomplished for each.

6.4   Verification of Purchased Product

This section states that even if your customer performs audit or inspection, you are still responsible for delivering a quality product. No checklist questions are necessary here.

7   Purchaser Supplied Product

1 Are there written procedures for verification, storage, and maintenance of customer supplied product? (This includes material and subassemblies.) Are they being used?

2 If customer supplied products are lost, damaged, or otherwise unsuitable, is this reported back to the customer?

*Customize prior to use

8   **Product Identification and Traceability**

    1 Are there written procedures for identifying the product during all stages of production, delivery and installation? Are they being used?

    2 Do individual products (or batches) have a unique, recorded identification for traceability purposes? (This is not required, unless specified in the contract.)

9   **Process Control**

9.1   **General**

    1 Are production (and installation) processes which directly affect quality identified?

    2 Are there documented work instructions for each of these identified processes? (Some exceptions allowed—see ISO 9001.) Are they being used?

    3 Is suitable equipment used on each of these identified processes?

    4 Does a suitable working environment exist for each of these identified processes?

    5 Are these processes in compliance with reference standards and codes?

    6 Have important product and process characteristics been defined? Are they monitored during production and installation? (Things to consider include materials, software and computer systems, limits, equipment drift, and so on.)

    7 Are identified processes and equipment formally approved on the basis of documented criteria? (When required.)

    8 Are there written standards for and/or samples of criteria for workmanship for these identified processes?

9.2   **Special Processes**

    1 Have "special processes" been identified? (See ISO 9001 for definition.)

    2 Is continuous monitoring and/or compliance with documented requirements in place for special processes?

    3 Are these special processes themselves qualified?

    4 Do all "special processes" meet the requirements for "processes" (preceding section above)?

    5 Are records kept for qualified processes, equipment and personnel?

*Customize prior to use

10   Inspection and Testing

10.1   Receiving Inspection and Testing

1 Is incoming material inspected or otherwise verified as conforming to specified requirements prior to use or processing? (10.1.1) (Examples of ways to accomplish this include: statistical sampling and testing, test verification, performance evaluation and test, process capability results, supplier verification (Certificate of Compliance/Conformance), 100% inspection, preshipment (source) inspection, and supplier audit.)

2 Is verification of incoming material done in accordance with a quality plan or documented procedures? (10.1.1) (See list above for procedures to examine.)

3 When incoming material is released for urgent production purposes before verification, is it positively identified and recorded to permit immediate recall and replacement in the event of nonconformance to specified requirements? (10.1.2)

10.2   In-Process Inspection and Testing

1 Is in-process inspection, testing, and identification carried out? Is it done in accordance with the quality plan and/or documented procedures?

2 Is conformance with requirements established using in-process monitoring and control methods? (See also Process Controls above.)

3 Is product held until required inspections and tests have been completed?

4 When product is not held for required inspections and tests, are positive recall procedures in place?

5 Has it been established that positive recall procedures are reliable?

6 Is nonconforming product identified?

7 Select [number] in-process inspections and observe their performance to the above criteria.

10.3   Final Inspection and Testing

1 Do final inspection plans/procedures specify that finished product shall have passed earlier inspections and tests?

2 Is final inspection and/or testing carried out? Is it done in accordance with the quality plan or documented procedures?

*Customize prior to use

3 Do final testing and inspection results show evidence of conformance of the finished product to specified requirements?

4 Is finished product held until all required activities have been satisfactorily completed?

5 Is finished product held until final inspection and test data are available and authorized (reviewed and accepted)?

6 Examine documented results from [number] recent final inspections for conformance to the above criteria.

10.4 Inspection and Test Records

1 Is there evidence (records) that the finished product has passed the inspections and tests as defined by the acceptance criteria?

2 Are inspection and test records accessible (available)?

11 Inspection, Measuring, and Test Equipment

1 Have required product measurements been identified? (11a)

2 Has accuracy of these measurements been defined? (11a)

3 Has inspection, measurement, and test equipment been identified? Does this include on-line devices? (11b)

4 Has inspection, measurement, and test equipment (and devices) been calibrated? (11b)

5 Is this equipment adjusted at prescribed intervals, or prior to use, against certified equipment having a known valid relationship to nationally recognized standards? (11b)

6 Where no calibration standards exist, is the basis for calibration documented? (11b)

7 Are there written calibration procedures for each type of equipment/device? (11c)

8 Do calibration procedures include details of equipment type, identification number, location, frequency of checks, check method, acceptance criteria, and action to be taken when results are unsatisfactory? (11c)

9 Is there documented evidence which shows that equipment is capable of the accuracy and precision necessary? (11d)

10 Is calibration status shown (by sticker or record) for inspection, measurement, and test equipment? (11e)

11 Do calibration records exist for each piece of equipment or device? Are they maintained? (11f)

*Customize prior to use

12 Is the validity of previous results assessed and documented when equipment is found to be out of calibration? (11g)

13 Are calibrations, inspections, measurements, and tests being carried out under suitable environmental conditions? (11h) (Consult manufacturer's information sheets for criteria.)

14 Is the handling, preservation, and storage of this equipment such that accuracy and fitness for use is maintained? (11i)

15 Are there safeguards against adjustments which would invalidate calibration settings? (11j)

16 Select [number] devices and attempt to trace their calibration back to the National Institute of Standards and Technology. When doing this, observe application and storage conditions as well as labeling and marking.

17 Is test hardware (jigs, patterns, and so on) and/or software used for inspection?

18 Are these hardware/software items checked to prove that they are capable of verifying the acceptability of product prior to use?

19 Are these hardware/software items rechecked at prescribed intervals? Has the extent and frequency of these capability checks been defined?

20 Are records of these hardware/software capability checks maintained?

12   Inspection and Test Status

1 Is there a way to indicate the conformance/nonconformance of product with regard to previous inspection and tests performed? (Typical indicators include markings, stamps, tags, labels, routing (traveler) cards, inspection records, test software, or physical location.)

2 Is the identification of this status maintained throughout production and installation?

3 Is there a record of who (inspection authority) releases conforming product.

13   Control of Nonconforming Product

1 Are there written procedures to prevent nonconforming (off-specification) product from inadvertent use or installation? Are they being used?

*Customize prior to use

2 Is nonconforming product identified, documented, evaluated, segregated (where practical), and dispositioned (see below)?

3 Are affected people (functions) notified of nonconforming product?

13.1 Nonconformity Review and Disposition

1 Is the responsibility and authority for review of nonconforming product defined?

2 Are there written procedures for the review of nonconforming product? Are they being used?

3 Do procedures for review of nonconforming product cover disposition by 1) rework to meet specified requirements, 2) acceptance (with or without repair) by concession, 3) regrading for alternative applications, or 4) rejection or scrapping?

4 Is the proposed use or repair of nonconforming product reported for concession (agreement) to the customer? (This may not be required by contract.)

5 Do recorded descriptions of accepted nonconformities and repairs denote the actual condition?

6 Is repaired or reworked product re-inspected?

14 Corrective Action

1 Are there written procedures for corrective action? Are they being used?

2 Do corrective action procedures require identification of the cause of nonconforming product and taking action to prevent (or minimize) recurrence? (14a)

3 Are there written procedures for analyzing all processes, work operations, all concessions, quality records, service reports, and customer complaints to detect and eliminate potential causes of nonconforming product? (14b) (This is sometimes referred to as "trend analysis.") Are they being used?

4 Are corrective actions taken? Are they effective? (14d)

5 Are procedures changed as a result of corrective action? (14e)

15 Handling, Storage, Packaging, and Delivery

15.1 General

1 Are there written procedures for handling, storage, packaging, and delivery of product? Are they being used?

*Customize prior to use

15.2 Handling

    1 Is product handled in ways that prevent damage and/or deterioration? This could include product containers as well. Also, be alert for potential sources of product contamination.

15.3 Storage

    1 Are secure storage areas or stock rooms provided which prevent damage or deterioration pending use or delivery?

    2 Are methods stipulated for receipt and dispatch to/from storage or stock rooms?

    3 Is the condition of stock assessed at periodic intervals to assess deterioration? Potential sources include vibration, shock, abrasion, corrosion, humidity and temperature. Be alert for limited shelf-life products.

15.4 Packaging

    1 Are the packing, preservation, and marking processes controlled?

    2 Is all product identified, preserved, and segregated from time of receipt to end of responsibility?

15.5 Delivery

    1 Are there provisions for the protection of product quality after final inspection and test?

    2 Does this protection include delivery to destination? (Only when required by contract.)

16 Quality Records

    1 Are there written procedures for identifying, collecting, indexing, filing, storing, maintaining, and disposing of quality records? Are they being used?

    2 Are quality records generated and maintained?

    3 Are subcontractor quality records a part of the quality records?

    4 Are quality records legible and identifiable to the product involved?

    5 Are quality records stored so that they are readily retrievable?

    6 Are quality records stored so as to minimize deterioration or damage and prevent loss?

    7 Are retention times for quality records established and recorded?

*Customize prior to use

8 Where agreed contractually, are quality records available for evaluation by the purchaser? How long?

9 Records are required in many sections of the standard. Verify that records for the following exist:
   * Management reviews of the quality system (1.3)
   * Contract reviews (3)
   * Design verification reviews (4.5)
   * Suppliers and subcontractors performance (6.2)
   * Acceptable suppliers and subcontractors (6.2)
   * Unsuitable purchaser-supplied product (7)
   * Product identification for batches or units, when required (8)
   * Special process qualification (process, equipment, personnel) (9.2)
   * Nonconforming material released for production (10.1.2)
   * Verification data that the product passed inspection/test (10.4)
   * Equipment calibration status (11e)
   * Inspection, measuring, and test equipment calibration (11f)
   * Test hardware/software validation (11)
   * Inspection authority for release of conforming product (12)
   * Nonconformance repair or accept-as-made (13.1)
   * Changes resulting from corrective action (14)
   * Personnel training (18)

10 Examine the records list for a specific type (model number) of product. Attempt to locate (touch) those records from [years] ago.

17   Internal Quality Audits

1 Are internal quality audits performed?

2 Do internal audits verify whether quality activities comply with planned arrangements?

3 Do internal audits evaluate the effectiveness of the quality system?

4 Are audits planned and scheduled? (The schedule will depend on the basis of the status and importance of the activities to be audited.)

5 Are audits and follow up actions carried out in accordance with written procedures?

*Customize prior to use

6 Are the results of audits documented and brought to the attention of personnel having responsibility in the area studied?

7 Is corrective action taken on any deficiencies found by the audit?

8 Examine [number] audits performed within the past [year] for conformance to the above.

18 Training

1 Are there written procedures for identifying training needs for activities affecting quality? Have "activities affecting quality" been defined?

2 Is identified training provided for all personnel performing activities affecting quality?

3 Are personnel performing specific assigned tasks qualified on the basis of appropriate education, training, and/or experience?

4 Are records of training maintained?

5 Select [number] people from each of [production, support, and QA/QC] groups. Attempt to verify that training needs were defined and accomplished for those specific individuals.

19 Servicing

1 Are there written procedures for performing and verifying specified service requirements? This only applies when servicing is specified in the contract.

20 Statistical Techniques

1 Have statistical techniques (required for verifying the acceptability of process capability and product characteristics) been identified? (Where appropriate.)

Index